THE
BREAD MACHINE
BOOK

THE BREAD MACHINE BOOK

OVER 100 RECIPES FOR EASY–TO–MAKE,

SPECTACULAR BREADS

MARJIE LAMBERT

FIREFLY BOOKS

Dedicated to Sarah, Diane and Beverley

A FIREFLY BOOK

Published in Canada by
Firefly Books Ltd.
3680 Victoria Park Avenue
Willowdale, Ontario M2H 3KI

Reprinted 1998

Canadian Cataloguing in Publication Data

Lambert, Marjie L., 1954
Bread machine book
Includes index
ISBN 1-55209-160-0

1. Bread   2. Automatic bread machines,   3. Cookery (Bread).
1. Title
TX769.L35 1997   641.8'15   C97-930741-4

This book was designed and produced by
Quintet Publishing Limited
6 Blundell Street, London N7 9BH

Creative Director: Richard Dewing
Designers: Ian Hunt; Linda Henley
Projct Editor: Alison Bravington
Editor: Janet Swarbrick
Photographer: David Armstrong

Typeset in Great Britain by
Central Southern Typesetters, Eastbourne
Manufactured in Malaysia by C. H. Colour Scan Sdn. Bhd.
Printed in Singapore by Star Standard Industries (Pte) Ltd

The publishers would like to thank
Panasonic for their help and for the loan
of a bread machine to create the
breads photographed.

CONTENTS

INTRODUCTION

This is a secret that for years I've tried to share with friends who cook, but it was a secret no one believed: baking bread is fun and easy. Time-consuming, yes. Messy, definitely. Kneading, while mentally relaxing, will tire your muscles. But difficult? No.

Bread dough is patient, flexible, and tolerant of mistakes. The rewards are wonderful – the fragrance, the texture, the taste of fresh-baked bread are unbeatable. But because people are often intimidated by the mysteries of yeast, bread-making at home has been in danger of becoming a lost art.

Using a bread machine, baking bread becomes one of the easiest tasks in the kitchen, yet it produces spectacular results. You don't have to worry that water will be too cold to activate yeast, or so hot that it kills it: the bread machine regulates the temperature. You won't be kneading dough until your muscles ache: the bread machine will do all the kneading for you. There's no need to worry that drafts from the air-conditioning unit will interfere with rising dough: the dough is protected while it's inside the machine. From a dark, dense pumpernickel to feather-light white bread to a sweet panettone, making a delicious array of breads is no more work than simply measuring out the ingredients. And since most machines have timers, the ingredients can be measured into the bread pan just before you go to bed and the freshly cooked bread will be hot when you wake up.

With a bread machine, you can create an infinite variety of loaves to suit your tastes, your pantry cupboard, and the season. Substitute dried cranberries for raisins in a Christmas bread, add cracked wheat to a favorite bread to give it more fiber, or decorate a braided loaf with the slivered almonds left over from another baking project. You no longer have to settle for ordinary bread.

Bread machines do have their flaws. Most are inflexible in their kneading, rising, and baking cycles; they purée fruits and nuts that are added at the beginning of the kneading cycle; and they have little tolerance for dough that is particularly stiff or soft. But the newer models have different settings for different varieties of bread – whole-wheat bread needs more time to rise than white bread; sweet breads need less baking time.

And if your bread machine still doesn't give you enough flexibility, you can just let the machine do the kneading, then remove it from the machine and let it rise and bake according to your timetable.

GETTING TO KNOW YOUR MACHINE

Mastering bread-machine baking is like getting to know the quirks and idiosyncrasies of any new piece of equipment. Some machines knead longer than others or allow longer rising time. Some bread pans have different capacities than others, although they are labeled as the same size. Some models require a little more liquid or yeast than others. Flour absorbs varying amounts of liquid depending on the weather. The dough reacts differently to water that is highly acidic or alkaline.

To get accustomed to a new machine or this book, start with a simple recipe, such as basic white bread, and see how it comes out. If you have any problems, refer to the Troubleshooting Guide on pages 14–15.

VIEWING WINDOW

LID

CONTROL PANEL

HANDLE

MEASURING CUP

BREAD PAN

KNEADING PADDLE

BAKING BREAD

Before you start, assemble all the ingredients. Be sure that the yeast is fresh. All ingredients should be at room temperature. Cold liquids and butter can be heated in the microwave (I usually add the butter to the liquid and heat them together). Hold a cold egg in your hand for five minutes or so while you review the recipe, or put it in a bowl of water no hotter than 80°F. Although frozen yeast should be given time to come to room temperature, yeast that has been stored in the refrigerator will come to room temperature quickly enough without special treatment. Never put yeast in the microwave.

Be sure the kneading paddle is well seated in the bottom of the pan. Add the ingredients in the order suggested by the manufacturer's instructions. This may vary from one machine to the next. If you are using a timer, the order may change; see "Using the Timer," below. Fit the bread pan securely into the bread machine. Select settings on the control panel according to the manufacturer's instructions and press "Start."

To check the dough while the bread is kneading, look for it to form a fairly smooth ball that is a bit tacky to the touch and settles only slightly when the paddle stops kneading. If, after the ingredients are mixed, the imprint of the paddle remains in the dough and the edges look a little jagged, add more liquid. Start with one tablespoon, then add additional liquid one teaspoon at a time, giving the dough time to absorb the liquid before adding more. If the dough is so soft that it loses its shape as soon as the paddle pauses, add more flour, one tablespoon at a time. Although these instructions fit most breads, some breads are designed to have dough that is a little stiffer or softer.

Don't be shy about keeping the lid up and watching at this stage. It is only when the bread is in the rising and baking stages that an open lid will interfere with temperature controls.

When the bread is done, remove it from the machine and the baking pan immediately. Otherwise, the steam released by the bread will condense in the pan, making the bread soggy on the outside. The bread should be allowed to cool for 20 to 30 minutes before you slice into it.

The kneading paddle should be well seated in the bottom of the bread pan.

Add ingredients in the order suggested by the manufacturer.

The bread pan should be securely seated inside the machine.

ADDITIONS

Fruit and vegetables added at the beginning of the knead cycle will be puréed or shredded into tiny pieces. If you want the raisins to remain whole or other fruit to remain in chunks, add it 10 to 15 minutes into the kneading cycle. Most machines now have a beeper that signals when it's time to add the additions.

If you are using the timer to make the bread and have no choice but to add all ingredients at the beginning, consider the moisture content of the additions. Juicy dried apricots or roasted red peppers may add as much as one or two tablespoons of juice if they go through the entire kneading process. Also, because too much sugar can interfere with the yeast, high-sugar additions like candied fruit should be added late in the kneading cycle.

USING THE TIMER

If you are using the bread machine timer so that the mixing will be delayed, the ingredients should be layered so the yeast does not come into contact with liquids prematurely. Generally, you should put the liquids in first, followed by the dry ingredients, and the yeast last. Salt and wheat germ may also interfere with the yeast if any significant quantities are in prolonged contact with the yeast.

Recipes containing perishable ingredients such as eggs or cottage cheese should not be made using the timer, unless the delay is only an hour or so. You can substitute water and powdered milk for whole milk (use three tablespoons of dry milk per 8 ounces), but the dry milk should be layered with the other dry ingredients so that it does not come in contact with the water prematurely. I have not had any trouble using small quantities of butter in bread made overnight. However, if you wish, you can substitute vegetable oil for butter.

OVEN-BAKED BREAD

Any of the breads in this cookbook can be baked in a conventional oven. I use a 9½-inch loaf pan for most breads. The 1½-pound breads made with bread flour may require a larger pan. The 1-pound breads that include rye or low-gluten flours can be cooked in the 9½-inch pan, but will rise higher and look more attractive in an 8½-inch pan. Unless otherwise indicated, most breads should be baked at 350°F for 30 to 35 minutes.

A cautionary note about baking sheets and bread pans: many of the pans available today are of a construction or material that changes the cooking conditions. Double-layered pans with an insulating air cushion protect against scorching, but bread cooked in these pans will take longer to bake. Some of the heavy, expensive pans with black surfaces will brown the bread faster and need lower baking temperatures and/or shorter baking times. If you use a glass loaf pan, reduce the oven temperature by 25°F.

ABOVE Bagels (page 85)

BREAD BAKING INGREDIENTS

People have been baking bread since prehistoric times, beginning with an unleavened bread made of meal ground from corns or beechnuts and mixed with water. The first leavened bread is believed to have been baked by the Egyptians about 4,000 B.C. Some dough left out for hours captured wild yeast from the air. When the dough was put on the hearth to bake, it puffed up. That was the first sourdough, although bakers went to great lengths to minimize the sour taste while taking advantage of its leavening qualities. Later, bakers discovered a yeasty byproduct of beer brewing that did not create such a sour taste. It was not until the 19th century that compressed yeast was perfected.

In basic bread, the yeast, activated by warm water and fed by sugar, ferments. It creates tiny bubbles of carbon dioxide gas that makes the dough rise. Gluten, an elastic protein in the dough, stretches and holds in the gas bubbles. The more gluten in the flour, the better the bread will rise.

FLOUR

Barley, millet, oats, rye, and wheat have been milled for thousands of years in Europe and Asia. Corn was a grain of the Americas. Only wheat and, to a lesser extent, rye, have the gluten necessary to make leavened bread. The other grains should be used in combination with wheat flour to make bread.

WHEAT FLOURS

Wheat flours, the most commonly used flours, are milled from the wheat berry. The berry consists of three parts: the outer hull, or bran; the small germ or embryo inside; and the endosperm, a starchy material that feeds the embryo.

White flour – including bread flour and all-purpose flour – consists of the milled endosperm, with the bran and germ removed. All-purpose flour is milled to be used in a variety of ways and is made with a combination of hard and soft wheats. Bread flour, milled specifically for bread, is made only from hard wheat. Bread flour has a higher gluten content and will absorb more liquid. Bread made with bread flour will rise significantly higher than bread made with all-purpose flour.

Whole-wheat flour contains the bran, germ, and endosperm of the wheat berry. It has proportionately less gluten than bread flour or all-purpose flour. It rises more slowly and not as high. It may also have a slightly bitter flavor. For those reasons, many whole-wheat breads are made with a combination of whole-wheat and white flours. Some bakers add wheat gluten for a higher loaf.

Graham flour, named after Dr. Sylvester Graham, a 19th-century health-food devotee, is a coarsely ground whole-wheat flour milled from soft winter wheat. It has less gluten than whole-wheat flour and will not rise as high. The quality of graham flour varies widely. Some manufacturers package inferior flour with wheat bran and label it graham flour.

Semolina flour is a high-gluten white flour milled from durum or hard winter wheat. It is most often used in pasta (and may be labeled pasta flour). It makes a delicious bread when used with other flour. By itself, it makes a heavy loaf.

Triticale is a man-made grain, a hybrid of rye and wheat. It is a high-protein grain with the hardiness of rye and the gluten of wheat, although it is best combined with wheat flour. This grain was created with the intent of cultivating it in difficult growing conditions in poorer parts of the world.

ABOVE Panettone (page 123)

NON-WHEAT FLOURS

Non-wheat flours are low in gluten or gluten-free and should be used in combination with wheat flours unless you require gluten-free bread for health reasons.

Rye is a hardy grain that grows well in cold, wet climates where wheat does not. That's why so many Scandinavian and Russian breads are rye breads. Rye flour contains some gluten, but must be mixed with wheat flour. Medium or light rye flour consists only of the endosperm. Dark rye and pumpernickel are milled from the bran, germ, and endosperm of the rye berry and are coarser, darker flours. Its grind and content may vary; some manufacturers market a blend of whole wheat and dark rye as pumpernickel.

Amaranth flour was a staple of the Aztecs. It has a nutty, slightly spicy flavor. It is higher in protein than most flours, but is low in gluten.

Barley flour, milled from a grain that dates back to the Stone Age, has a slightly sweet taste, a soft texture, and a low gluten content.

Buckwheat flour is made from the triangular seeds of a cereal grass. It adds a pungent, earthy flavor to bread. It is a high-fat flour, low in gluten.

Corn flour, milled from the whole kernel of corn, adds a sweet flavor to bread. It is gluten-free. Corn starch and British cornflour are milled only from the endosperm.

Millet flour, milled since Neolithic times and a staple food in parts of Africa and Asia, adds a yellowish color and a pleasantly gritty texture to bread. It is low in gluten.

Oat flour, made from oats that have been ground into powder, is very low in gluten and must be mixed with wheat flour, but is high in protein.

Quinoa flour, an ancient pearly grain from Peru, gives bread a nutty flavor. It is very high in protein and is gluten-free.

Rice flour, the flour most commonly used in gluten-free breads, is milled from either white or brown rice. It makes bread with a sweet flavor and chewy texture. Brown rice flour includes the bran.

Soybean flour gives bread a moist texture and is very high in protein, but should be used sparingly because it adds a slight bitter flavor. It is gluten-free.

GRAINS

A few of these grains are easily found in grocery stores, but most will be found only in health-food stores. They will add taste and texture to bread, but will not contribute to its rising. They should be added in small quantities, typically 2 to 4 tablespoons for a 1-pound loaf.

WHEAT

Many forms of wheat are available as grains. The wheat berry is the whole grain, and it is much too hard to eat as it is. It can be softened by sprouting (the berry is soaked in water that is changed at least twice a day for several days) or by cooking (the berry is boiled with lots of water for an hour).

Cracked wheat is the wheat berry that has been broken into pieces, but is still too hard to eat without cooking. It can be softened by boiling for 30 to 40 minutes.

Bulgur is a wheat berry that has been steamed and cracked. It adds crunch to bread. To cook bulgur, boil in water for six minutes and drain thoroughly.

Wheat bran, the outer hull of the grain, is also known as miller's bran or unprocessed bran flakes. It interferes with the elasticity of gluten and should be used in small quantities.

Wheat germ is the embryo of the wheat berry. It is high in nutrients, has a nutty flavor, and is high in oils which can cause it to turn rancid if it is not kept refrigerated.

Bran cereals, such as bran flakes or All-Bran, are made with wheat bran and other ingredients, including sugar and salt, and may be toasted. They add good flavor and texture to bread.

OTHER GRAINS

Cornmeal, milled from corn, adds a sweet flavor and, if uncooked, a crumbly texture. It can interfere with the gluten, so should be used in small quantities unless it is cooked or softened in boiling water first.

Millet, widely used as birdseed, can be added to bread in small amounts in its whole, unhulled state.

Oatmeal, the most nutritious of the cereal grasses, means old-fashioned rolled oats in this cookbook. The husk is removed and the grain is sliced, steamed, and rolled. The dried oats may have trouble absorbing thicker liquids such as applesauce or buttermilk. In this cookbook, most recipes using those liquids call for a little boiling water to be poured over the oatmeal before other ingredients are added.

Oat bran is the hull of the oat and is high in soluble fiber. Oat bran can interfere with the gluten in bread dough and should be used in small quantities, between 2 and 4 ounces for a 1-pound loaf.

YEAST

Yeast is a living organism that is activated when it comes in contact with warm liquids. It ferments most readily when it has sugar to feed on, which is why most bread recipes contain at least a teaspoon of sugar. However, it will also feed on flour.

In this book, yeast means active dry yeast. I had the best results with a yeast made specifically for bread machines and sold in 4-ounce jars. Yeast in pre-measured envelopes also worked, although the bread did not rise as high. I also tested a rapid-rise yeast, and it worked nicely on the bread machine's rapid-bake cycle, but it rose the least of all four yeasts I tested. Because the whole-wheat flour needs a longer rising period, I wouldn't recommend using a quick-rise yeast when you make whole-wheat bread.

SALT

Salt is critical in bread. It strengthens the gluten. Salt-free bread may rise nicely, but will then collapse. However, salt in high concentrations also inhibits the yeast's rising action. Salt and yeast should never be added so that they come in contact with each other prior to mixing. Because some sodium is necessary for bread, most salt substitutes cannot be used.

SWEETENERS

Yeast ferments best when it feeds on sugar. Sugar also acts as a preservative and contributes to the golden color of the crust. But too much sugar will interfere with the yeast's rising action and cause the bread to collapse. Most yeast breads and rolls are not very sweet, even if they are dessert breads. Dessert breads usually get their sweetness from a glaze, dry sugar topping, or another addition which is made after baking.

The addition of candied fruit is a particular problem with bread machines. When candied fruit is used, it is usually in breads that already have several tablespoons of sweetener. The kneading will shred the candied fruit and release more sugar into the dough. Candied fruit should be added late in the kneading cycle, or kneaded in by hand if the bread is to be baked in the oven.

Sugar also scorches easily. A growing number of machines have a special setting with shorter cooking times for sweet breads. If your machine does not have a sweet-bread setting, choose the light-crust option.

In small quantities – 1 or 2 tablespoons – sugar, brown sugar, honey, and molasses can be substituted for each other in equal amounts. Sugar and brown sugar can always be substituted for each other. Tablespoon for tablespoon, most honeys are slightly sweeter than sugar. If the recipe calls for more than two tablespoons of sweetener, substitute two parts honey for three parts sugar (e.g., 2 tablespoons of honey for 3 tablespoons of sugar). Molasses is not as sweet as sugar. When substituting more than two tablespoons, use four parts molasses for three parts sugar. Confectioner's sugar contains cornstarch and should not be used as a substitute.

Less commonly used sweeteners in bread are maple syrup and corn syrup. Maple syrup can be substituted in equal quantities. Corn syrup is not as sweet as sugar and should be substituted with two parts corn syrup for one part sugar.

Liquid forms of sugar, including honey, molasses, corn syrup, and maple syrup, should be counted toward the total liquid content of the ingredients. If the substitution involves substituting a dry form for a liquid form, or vice versa, you will need to adjust the liquid ingredients accordingly.

LIQUIDS

The variety of liquids used in bread-baking is nearly infinite. Most common are water, milk, buttermilk, eggs, beer, and potato water, but don't be surprised to come across recipes that list wine, orange juice, or other liquids. Sour cream, yogurt, and cottage cheese should be counted as liquids, although their consistencies differ and the amount of other liquid needed may vary. Puréed fruit and vegetables such as applesauce and mashed potatoes also contain some liquid. Water that potatoes have been cooked in adds flavor, nutrients, and a softer texture to bread.

Water will give the bread a crisper crust. Most tap water is fine, but soft (acidic) water may produce soft, sticky dough, and hard (alkaline) water will interfere with the fermentation of the yeast.

Milk will give the bread a softer crust and more golden color. You can substitute equal amounts of whole, skimmed, and non-fat milk for each other.

Powdered non-fat milk is very helpful in bread-baking, particularly when the bread is being baked on a timer and the ingredients will be sitting at room temperature overnight. Powdered milk is also used when the recipe calls for another liquid – such as beer or applesauce – but you still want a golden color and softer crust. Use 3 tablespoons of powdered milk per cup of liquid.

Buttermilk will give the bread a tender crumb and a hint of tangy flavor. It also adds to the acidity of the dough and may need to be neutralized with a pinch of baking soda.

EGGS

Eggs give bread a softer crust and richer flavor and contribute to the leavening. In this cookbook, breads were tested using large eggs, which are equal to about 2 ounces of liquid. I generally avoided recipes that call for only part of an egg, and increased other liquids by 2 tablespoons instead. When the bread's eggy character is important, though, recipes will call for an extra yolk. Breads containing eggs should not be made on a timer unless the delay is no more than one hour.

FATS

Fats are used sparingly in most breads, but are important. They act as preservatives and give a tender texture. French bread goes stale quickly because it uses no fat. Butter, margarine, vegetable oil, shortening, and lard can be used interchangeably. In small quantities there will be no noticeable difference. If you are substituting more than one tablespoon of a solid fat for a liquid fat or vice versa, the amount of other liquid in the dough will have to be adjusted.

Lard gives bread a slightly flakier texture and crustier finish. I don't like to use margarine because it can contain water. If you're watching cholesterol and want a substitute for butter, use vegetable oil. You can substitute olive oil; in quantities less than three tablespoons, you are not likely to notice a difference in taste, especially if you're not using extra-virgin olive oil. Specialty oils, such as sesame and walnut oil, are strongly flavored and should be used sparingly.

If you want to cut every bit of fat out of your bread, you can substitute applesauce or puréed prunes. Puréed fruit contains some liquid, so the amount of other liquid in the recipe may have to be reduced.

Butter should always be brought to room temperature before the dough is kneaded. Soft butter mixes more evenly. This is especially critical in high-fat breads like brioche.

A note about greasing baking sheets or pans: use butter or solid vegetable shortening. Oil will soak into the dough. Some margarines may scorch.

TROUBLESHOOTING GUIDE

TOO MUCH OR TOO LITTLE LIQUID

The most frequent cause of trouble with bread made in a bread machine is too much or too little liquid. Keep in mind that flour absorbs moisture from the air. That's why a loaf of bread may turn out perfect one time and awful the next. In humid weather, the flour may have already absorbed an extra 1 or 2 tablespoons of moisture. If you add the usual amount of liquid, it may mushroom and collapse, or develop a coarse, holey texture. Likewise, if the climate is very dry, the flour may need a little extra moisture, or it will have a dense, heavy texture or a gnarled top.

Check the dough about 10 minutes into the kneading cycle. The dough should be smooth, soft, and slightly tacky. It should settle just the slightest bit, but hold its shape when the kneading paddle stops. If the dough is very soft, settles quickly when the kneading paddle stops, and can't hold its shape, add 1 tablespoon of flour. If the dough is stiff with ragged edges and imprints of the paddle remain in the dough for more than a couple of seconds, add 1 tablespoon of liquid.

TEMPERATURE

Ingredients should be at room temperature. But "room temperature" may be too hot or too cold in particularly hot or cold weather. If the ingredients are too cold, they may not activate the yeast soon enough. If they are too warm – such as on a hot day in a kitchen that is not air-conditioned – the yeast may cause the dough to rise too much and overflow the machine.

ADDING FRUIT AND VEGETABLES

Another variable that can put too much liquid into the dough is fruit or vegetables. If fruit or vegetables are added at the beginning of the kneading cycle, they will be ground up and release more liquid than if they were added at the beeper or after the first kneading. If you're using the timer to knead the bread, have to add fruit or vegetables at the beginning, and can't check the dough during the kneading, reduce liquids by 1 to 2 teaspoons for drier additions like raisins or sun-dried tomatoes, and by 1 to 2 tablespoons for wetter additions, like shredded apple or roasted red peppers.

PROBLEMS AND ANSWERS

BREAD COLLAPSED

- Too much liquid. Next time reduce liquid by 2 tablespoons, then monitor the dough as it kneads and adjust liquid or flour for a firm but sticky dough.
- You omitted the salt or used a salt substitute. The gluten needs some salt to support it as it rises. Minimum amount is ½ teaspoon for a 1-pound loaf, ¾ teaspoon for a 1½-pound loaf. Most salt substitutes will not work.
- Too much sugar. Decrease by 1 tablespoon next time. You're getting into dangerous territory with more than ¼ cup sugar for a 1-pound loaf, 6 tablespoons for a 1½-pound loaf, although some recipes will work with more. Don't forget that sugary additions like candied fruit increase the quantity of sugar.

BREAD HAS BURNED CRUST, BUT CENTER IS FINE

- Too much sugar can cause the crust to burn. Set controls for sweet bread and/or light crust. If it still burns – or your machine does not have those settings – reduce sugar (or other sweetener) by 1 tablespoon. Or remove the bread 5 minutes before the machine is done. Or bake the bread in a loaf pan in a conventional oven.

BREAD NOT BAKED IN CENTER

- Too much liquid or not enough flour. Next time, reduce liquid by 1 to 2 tablespoons or increase flour by 2 to 4 tablespoons (if the bread pan has room for a larger loaf); then monitor dough as it kneads, and adjust flour or liquid for a firm but sticky dough. The bread machine has little tolerance for dough that varies much from a set ratio of liquid to flour. Often, those same breads – especially sweet breads like kugelhopf or panettone – will turn out fine when baked in a conventional oven. Set the bread machine to make dough, then remove it, punch it down, and put it in a buttered loaf pan. Let it rise in a warm place for 45 minutes to 1 hour, then bake at 375°F for about 30 minutes.
- If it is a sweet bread and has sticky pockets, reduce the sugar or sweetener by 1 tablespoon.

TROUBLESHOOTING GUIDE

BREAD HAS GNARLED TOP AND/OR HEAVY, DENSE TEXTURE

- Not enough liquid or too much flour. If the bread pan has room for a larger loaf, add 1 to 2 tablespoons of liquid next time; otherwise, reduce flour by 2 to 4 tablespoons. Monitor dough as it kneads and adjust liquid or flour for a firm but sticky texture. (Note: If you tap the measuring cup several times to get flour to settle, you may be cramming too much flour into the measuring cup.)
- Too much low-gluten flour. Breads that consist entirely of rye or, to a lesser extent, whole-wheat flour will be dense and heavy. Sometimes, this is desirable. If it is not, substitute bread flour for part of the rye or whole-wheat flour. Or add wheat gluten, an additive available at health-food stores.
- Too many extras, such as oatmeal, wheat germ, fruit, or nuts substituted for flour. If there is room in your bread pan, add 2 ounces bread flour and about 2 tablespoons of liquid. Otherwise, reduce the extras.
- Dry grains soaked up too much liquid. Oatmeal is a particular offender. Add 1 to 2 tablespoons of liquid.

BREAD HAS MUSHROOM TOP WITH AIR UNDERNEATH, OR HAS TUNNELS OR COARSE HOLEY TEXTURE

- Too much liquid. Next time, reduce the amount of liquid by 1 to 2 tablespoons, then monitor the dough as it kneads and adjust the amount of liquid or flour for a firm but sticky dough.
- Too much yeast. Reduce yeast by ¼ teaspoon for a smaller loaf, ½ teaspoon for a larger loaf.

BREAD RISES TOO MUCH

- Too much yeast. Reduce the amount of yeast by ½ teaspoon next time.
- Too much liquid, especially if there are large air pockets in bread. Reduce liquid by 1 to 2 tablespoons next time, check kneading, and adjust flour for firm, sticky texture.
- You omitted the salt. Salt supports the gluten and stops it collapsing, but it also stops the yeast rising too high.

BREAD DOESN'T RISE ENOUGH

- Not enough yeast. Increase yeast by ½ teaspoon next time.
- Yeast is not fresh. Proof by putting 2 teaspoons of yeast in ½ cup warm water 105 to 115°F. If it does not develop a thick head of foam in 5 to 10 minutes, discard the yeast.
- You're using rapid-rise yeast or the rapid-rise cycle. The price for this shortcut is a loaf that doesn't rise as high.
- You're using yeast that does not do well in bread machines. Switch to yeast produced specifically for bread machines.
- You used hot liquid – over 115°F – and it killed the yeast.
- Not enough liquid. Increase liquid by 1 tablespoon next time.
- Too much sugar (honey, molasses, etc.) may be interfering with yeast. If it is a high-sugar bread (or if it has sugary additions like candied fruit), reduce sugar by 1 tablespoon, or increase yeast by ¼ teaspoon. Conversely, yeast works better when there is at least 1 teaspoon of sugar to feed it. Although some recipes, such as French Bread, get along without it, the yeast rises better with a small amount of sweetener.
- You're using too much low-gluten flour. Increase the proportion of white flour. Or substitute bread flour for all-purpose flour.
- Your tap water is too hard (alkaline). Add 1 teaspoon of lemon juice or vinegar.
- Too much salt. This may be because you added salty extras, like salted nuts, without reducing the amount of salt.
- You allowed the salt and yeast to come in contact with each other prior to mixing. A high concentration of salt in direct contact with yeast can kill the yeast.
- You opened the lid during the rising stage and allowed warm air to escape.

BREAD DOESN'T RISE AT ALL AND IS A STICKY OR BURNT LAYERED MESS

- You forgot to set the paddle in the pan, or it was not firmly seated and came loose.

Basic Breads

BASIC WHITE BREAD

This is an all-purpose white bread. It is a good basic recipe with which you can try different brands of flour and yeast, as well as experiment with slight variations in the amounts of ingredients.

1 lb LOAF	INGREDIENTS	1½ lb LOAF
½ cup	water	¾ cup
¼ cup	milk	6 tbsp
1 tbsp	butter	1½ tbsp
1 tbsp	sugar	1½ tbsp
1 tsp	salt	1½ tsp
2 cups	bread flour	3 cups
2 tsp	yeast	1 tbsp

METHOD

Put all ingredients in bread pan in order suggested by your bread machine instructions. Set for white bread, medium crust. Press Start.

HONEY WHEAT BREAD

This is a dense, slightly sweet bread with a high proportion of whole-wheat flour. It is good for toast or sandwiches.

1 lb LOAF	INGREDIENTS	1½ lb LOAF
½ cup	milk	¾ cup
¼ cup	water	6 tbsp
2 tbsp	butter	3 tbsp
2 tbsp	honey	3 tbsp
1 tbsp	sugar	1½ tbsp
¾ tsp	salt	1 tsp
1½ cups	whole-wheat flour	2¼ cups
½ cup	bread flour	¾ cup
2 tsp	yeast	1 tbsp

METHOD

Put ingredients in bread pan in order suggested by your bread machine instructions. Set for whole-wheat bread, medium crust. Press Start.

EGG BREAD

This is another all-purpose white bread, but the addition of egg gives it a subtly richer flavor and texture than basic white bread.

1 lb LOAF	INGREDIENTS	1½ lb LOAF
1	egg	1 + 1 yolk
½ cup	milk	¾ cup
1 tbsp	butter	1½ tbsp
2 tbsp	sugar	3 tbsp
1 tsp	salt	1½ tsp
2 cups	bread flour	3 cups
1½ tsp	yeast	2¼ tsp

METHOD

Put ingredients in bread pan in order suggested by your bread machine instructions. Set for white bread, medium crust. Press Start.

SOUR CREAM CORNMEAL BREAD

This bread is specifically for toast. Untoasted, it is dry. Thinly sliced, it makes excellent melba toast.

1 lb LOAF	INGREDIENTS	1½ lb LOAF
1	egg	1
2 tbsp	water	⅓ cup
½ cup	sour cream	¾ cup
2 tbsp	butter	3 tbsp
1 tbsp	sugar	1½ tbsp
½ tsp	salt	¾ tsp
¾ cup	cornmeal	⅞ cup
1½ cups	bread flour	2¼ cups
1½ tsp	yeast	2¼ tsp

METHOD

Put ingredients in bread pan in order suggested by your bread machine instructions. Set for white bread, medium crust. Press Start.

RIGHT Egg Bread

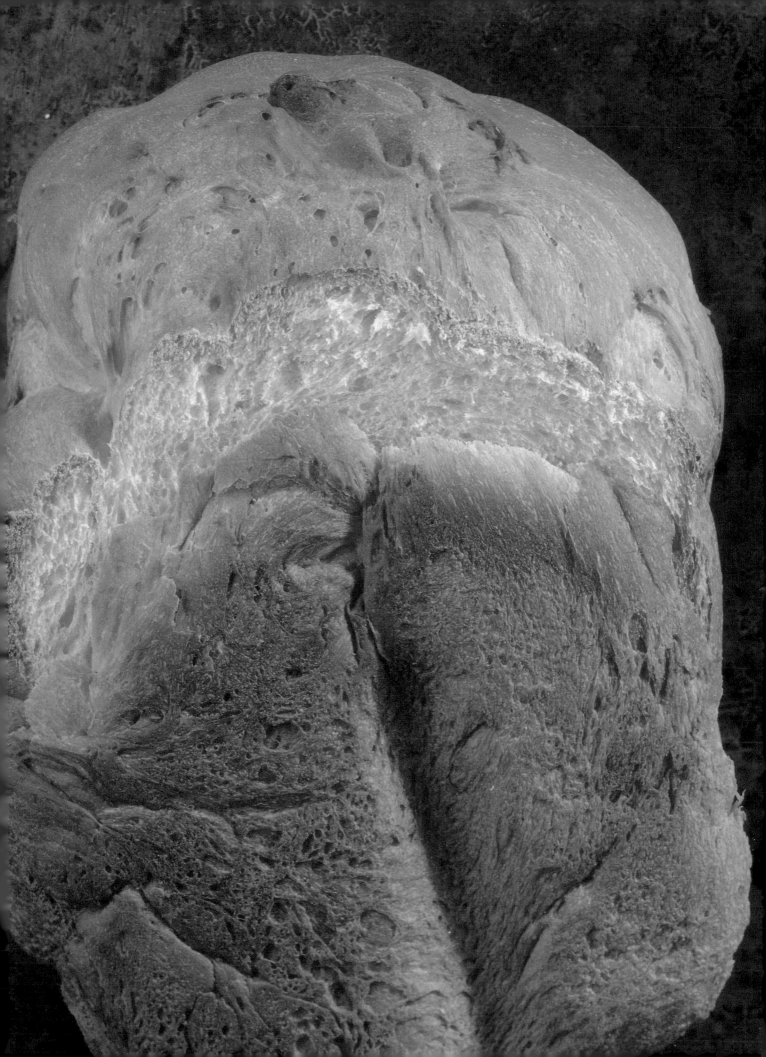

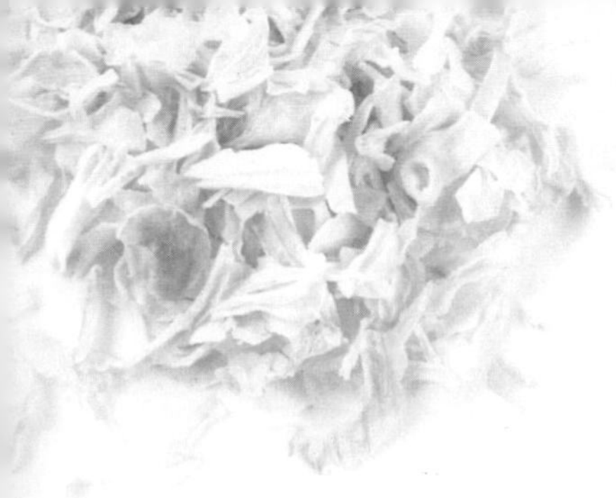

ONION DILL RYE BREAD

This is a strongly flavored rye bread, good for meat sandwiches.

1 lb LOAF	INGREDIENTS	1½ lb LOAF
¾ cup	water	1 cup
1 tbsp	vegetable oil	1½ tbsp
1 tbsp	sugar	1½ tbsp
1 tsp	salt	1½ tsp
2 tsp	dried dillweed	1 tbsp
2 tsp	dehydrated minced onion	1 tbsp
2 tbsp	cornmeal	3 tbsp
1⅓ cups	bread flour	2 cups
¾ cup	rye flour	1 cup + 2 tbsp
2 tsp	yeast	1 tbsp

METHOD

Put ingredients in bread pan in order suggested by your bread machine instructions. Set for whole-wheat bread, medium crust. Press Start.

LIGHT RYE BREAD

This light rye bread, made with beer, is lighter in color and texture than most rye breads. Mildly flavored, it is good for sandwiches.

1 lb LOAF	INGREDIENTS	1½ lb LOAF
¾ cup	flat beer	1¼ cups
1 tbsp	vegetable oil	1½ tbsp
1 tbsp	honey	1½ tbsp
1 tsp	salt	1½ tsp
1 tsp	caraway seeds	1½ tsp
1¼ cups	bread flour	1⅞ cups
1 cup	rye flour	1½ cups
2 tsp	yeast	1 tbsp

METHOD

Put ingredients in bread pan in order suggested by your bread machine instructions. Set for whole-wheat bread, medium crust. Press Start.

RIGHT Onion Dill Rye Bread

PUMPERNICKEL BREAD

This is an excellent bread for sandwiches or canapés.

1 lb LOAF	INGREDIENTS	1½ lb LOAF
¾ cup	milk	1¼ cups
1 tbsp	vegetable oil	1½ tbsp
2 tbsp	molasses	3 tbsp
½ tsp	salt	¾ tsp
2 tbsp	unsweetened cocoa powder	3 tbsp
2 tsp	caraway seeds	1 tbsp
⅓ cup	bread flour	½ cup
1 cup	rye flour	1½ cups
½ cup	whole-wheat flour	¾ cup
2 tbsp	cornmeal	3 tbsp
2 tsp	yeast	1 tbsp

METHOD

Put ingredients in bread pan in order suggested by your bread machine instructions. Set for whole-wheat bread, medium crust. Press Start.

Alternatively, to make baguettes, remove dough from bread machine after first kneading and punch down. Cut dough in two equal parts. Roll each part into a thick rope, about 8 inches long for the 1-pound recipe, 10 inches for the 1½-pound recipe. Put baguettes on a baking sheet that has been sprinkled with cornmeal. Put in a warm place and cover loosely. Let rise until doubled in volume. Bake in a preheated 350°F oven about 25 minutes, or until loaves are crusty and sound hollow.

BUTTERMILK PUMPERNICKEL BREAD

This is a dense, flavorful rye bread, good for sandwiches. The dough should be checked early in the kneading stage to see if more liquid or flour is needed.

1 lb LOAF	INGREDIENTS	1½ lb LOAF
½ cup	buttermilk	¾ cup
¼ cup	water	6 tbsp
1 tbsp	vegetable oil	1½ tbsp
2 tbsp	molasses	3 tbsp
1½ tsp	caraway seeds	2¼ tsp
¼ tsp	baking soda	¼ tsp
1 tsp	salt	1½ tsp
1½ cups	bread flour	2¼ cups
¾ cup	pumpernickel flour	1¼ cups
1½ tsp	yeast	2¼ tsp

METHOD

Put ingredients in bread pan in order suggested by your bread machine instructions. Set for whole-wheat bread, medium crust. Press Start.

BLACK PUMPERNICKEL

This is a very dense, very flavorful bread, made with a coarse grind of pumpernickel flour. Although the texture is lightened somewhat by the addition of mashed potatoes, it is not a high riser. It is delicious with sweet butter alone, but is also good for sandwiches. Because the grinds of pumpernickel flours vary widely, all breads may not have the same result.

1 lb LOAF	INGREDIENTS	1 ½ lb LOAF
¼ cup	cornmeal	6 tbsp
¼ cup	boiling water	6 tbsp
¼ cup	very strong coffee	6 tbsp
½ cup	mashed potatoes	¾ cup
2 tbsp	powdered milk	3 tbsp
2 tbsp	vegetable oil	3 tbsp
3 tbsp	molasses	4 ½ tbsp
1 tbsp	unsweetened cocoa	1 ½ tbsp
1 tsp	salt	1 ½ tsp
1 tsp	caraway seeds	1 ½ tsp
⅔ cup	pumpernickel flour	1 cup
1 ⅓ cups	bread flour	2 cups
1 ½ tsp	yeast	2 ¼ tsp

METHOD

Put cornmeal in bread pan and pour boiling water over it. Stir. Let cool 15 minutes. If the coffee is hot, add it immediately after stirring in the water. Otherwise, add it with the other ingredients. Put remaining ingredients in bread pan in order suggested by your bread machine instructions. Set for whole-wheat bread, medium crust. Press Start.

BEER MUSTARD BREAD

Although seasoned with mustard and thyme, this bread is more subtly flavored than you might expect. It goes well with meats, whether as a dinner bread or sandwich bread.

1 lb LOAF	INGREDIENTS	1½ lb LOAF
¾ cup	flat beer	1¼ cups
2 tbsp	powdered milk	3 tbsp
1 tbsp	vegetable oil	1½ tbsp
1 tbsp	sugar	1½ tbsp
2 tbsp	Dijon-style mustard	3 tbsp
½ tsp	dried thyme	¾ tsp
1 tsp	salt	1½ tsp
2 cups	bread flour	3 cups
1½ tsp	yeast	2¼ tsp

METHOD

Place all ingredients in bread pan in order recommended by your bread machine instructions. Set machine for white bread, medium crust. Press Start.

POTATO BREAD

Mashed potatoes add subtle flavor and texture to white bread. Use this as you would use ordinary white bread. Potatoes seasoned with garlic or herbs add a nice flavor to the bread.

1 lb LOAF	INGREDIENTS	1½ lb LOAF
½ cup	mashed potatoes	¾ cup
7 tbsp	potato water	⅔ cup
2 tbsp	vegetable oil	3 tbsp
1 tbsp	honey	1½ tbsp
1 tsp	salt	1½ tsp
2 cups	bread flour	3 cups
2 tsp	yeast	1 tbsp

METHOD

Put ingredients in bread pan in order suggested by your bread machine instructions. If you don't have the water the potatoes were boiled in, use plain water. Set for white bread, medium crust. Press Start.

The recipe is based on plain mashed potatoes – no milk, butter or salt. However, if you have leftover mashed potatoes with additions, just adjust the recipe slightly, for example by reducing the water by 1 tablespoon.

LEFT Beer Mustard Bread

GRAHAM BREAD

*Graham flour, a coarsely ground whole-wheat flour, gives this bread a
slightly chewy texture. Molasses subtly changes the flavor. It is good for
toast, grilled cheese sandwiches, or as a dinner bread.*

1 lb LOAF	INGREDIENTS	1½ lb LOAF
¾ cup	water	1¼ cups
1 tbsp	vegetable oil	1½ tbsp
2 tbsp	molasses	3 tbsp
½ tsp	salt	¾ tsp
1 cup	bread flour	1½ cups
1 cup	graham flour	1½ cups
1½ tsp	yeast	2¼ tsp

METHOD

Put ingredients in bread pan in order suggested by your
bread machine instructions. Set for whole-wheat bread,
medium crust. Press Start.

Rye Bread

This is a basic rye bread, good for sandwiches or as a dinner bread. It can be baked in the bread machine or in the oven.

1 lb LOAF	INGREDIENTS	1½ lb LOAF
¾ cup	water	1¼ cup
1 tbsp	vegetable oil	1½ tbsp
4 tsp	molasses	2 tbsp
1 tsp	salt	1½ tsp
2 tsp	caraway seeds	1 tbsp
1½ cups	bread flour	2¼ cups
¾ cup	rye flour	1 cup + 2 tbsp
2 tsp	yeast	1 tbsp

METHOD

Put ingredients in bread pan in order suggested by your bread machine instructions. Set for whole-wheat bread, medium crust. Press Start.

For oven-baked bread, set machine for dough stage. When dough is ready, remove it from the machine and press down. Shape it into a large ball and flatten it slightly. Or roll it into a fat baguette. Place it on a baking sheet that has been sprinkled with cornmeal. Cover the bread loosely, set it in a warm place, and let it rise until doubled in volume, about 1 hour.

Make a wash of 1 egg lightly beaten with 1 tablespoon of milk. Gently brush the egg wash over the top and sides of the loaf. Bake the bread in a preheated 375°F oven until the top and bottom are crusty and sound hollow when thumped – about 35 minutes.

Cornmeal Yeast Bread

Boiled cornmeal adds flavor to this pale yellow bread. It's good for toast, sandwiches, or just eaten warm with sweet butter.

1 lb LOAF	INGREDIENTS	1½ lb LOAF
1 cup	water	1½ cups
1 tsp	salt	1½ tsp
1½ tbsp	butter	2¼ tbsp
½ cup	cornmeal	¾ cup
¼ cup	milk	6 tbsp
1 tsp	sugar	1½ tbsp
1¾ cups	bread flour	2⅔ cups
1½ tsp	yeast	2¼ tsp

METHOD

Boil water in small saucepan. Add salt and butter. Then pour cornmeal in a thin stream, stirring constantly, until mixture forms a thick paste. Cook one minute longer, stirring all the while. Remove mixture from heat and set aside to cool.

When cornmeal paste has cooled, put it in the bread pan along with the other ingredients in the order suggested by your bread machine instructions. Set for white bread, medium crust. Press Start.

Buttermilk Oatmeal Bread

Oatmeal, wheat germ, and buttermilk give this bread a soft, loose texture and delicate flavor. It is delicious with cheese.

1 lb LOAF	INGREDIENTS	1½ lb LOAF
⅓ cup	very hot water	½ cup
½ cup	rolled oats (not quick oatmeal)	¾ cup
⅝ cup	buttermilk	1 cup
1 tbsp	butter	1½ tbsp
2 tbsp	sugar	3 tbsp
1 tsp	salt	1½ tsp
½ tsp	baking soda	½ tsp
2 tbsp	wheat germ	3 tbsp
1¾ cups	bread flour	2⅔ cups
1½ tsp	yeast	2¼ tsp

METHOD

Put oats in bread pan. Pour very hot or boiling water over the oats and stir. Let sit at least 15 minutes. Put remaining ingredients in bread pan in order suggested by your bread machine instructions. Set for white bread, medium crust. Press Start.

RIGHT Cornmeal Yeast Bread

ITALIAN HERB BREAD

This is a delicious white bread, seasoned with garlic and Italian herbs. It makes delicious cheese or meat sandwiches, and is an excellent dinner bread.

1 lb LOAF	INGREDIENTS	1½ lb LOAF
2 tbsp	olive oil	3 tbsp
1	clove garlic, pressed	1 or 2
1 tsp	dried basil	1½ tsp
½ tsp	dried oregano	¾ tsp
¼ tsp	dried rosemary	¼ tsp
¼ tsp	dried thyme	½ tsp
½ cup	water	¾ cup
¼ cup	milk	6 tbsp
1 tsp	sugar	1½ tsp
1 tsp	salt	1½ tsp
2 cups	bread flour	3 cups
1½ tsp	yeast	2¼ tsp

METHOD

Heat oil in a small skillet. Add the garlic and herbs. Saute for 2 minutes, taking care not to let the garlic scorch or it will turn bitter. If necessary, remove the pan from the stove. The herbs will continuing cooking in the oil's heat.

Put the herb oil and remaining ingredients in bread pan in order suggested by your bread machine instructions. Set for white bread, medium crust. Press Start.

ORANGE CUMIN BREAD

This light whole-wheat bread is slightly sweet and flavored with orange and cumin, a pungent spice frequently used in Mexican, Middle Eastern, Asian, and Mediterranean cooking. Try this bread with chicken or fish.

1 lb LOAF	INGREDIENTS	1½ lb LOAF
½ cup	milk	¾ cup
¼ cup	water	6 tbsp
2 tbsp	vegetable oil	3 tbsp
3 tbsp	sugar	4½ tbsp
1 tbsp	grated orange peel	1½ tbsp
¾ tsp	ground cumin	1¼ tsp
1 tsp	salt	1½ tsp
2 tbsp	cornmeal	3 tbsp
1½ cups	bread flour	2¼ cups
½ cup	whole-wheat flour	¾ cup
1½ tsp	yeast	2¼ tsp

METHOD

Put ingredients in bread pan in order suggested by your bread machine instructions. Set for whole-wheat bread, medium crust. Press Start.

BROWN SUGAR PECAN BREAD

This is a slightly sweet bread. Try it toasted with cream cheese.

1 lb LOAF	INGREDIENTS	1½ lb LOAF
½ cup	water	¾ cup
¼ cup	milk	6 tbsp
2 tbsp	butter	3 tbsp
3 tbsp	brown sugar	4½ tbsp
1½ tsp	cinnamon	2¼ tsp
½ tsp	salt	¾ tsp
¼ cup	oat bran	6 tbsp
2 cups	bread flour	3 cups
1½ tsp	yeast	2¼ tsp
½ cup	chopped pecans	¾ cup

METHOD

Put all ingredients except pecans in bread pan in order suggested by your bread machine instructions. Set for white bread, medium crust. Press Start. Add pecans after first kneading or when machine beeps to add fruit or nuts.

SALLY LUNN BREAD

Sally Lunn bread originated in Great Britain, but the southern United States has claimed it as its own. Traditionally, it is baked in a tube pan.

1 lb LOAF	INGREDIENTS	1½ lb LOAF
⅓ cup	milk	½ cup
2	eggs	3
¼ cup	butter	6 tbsp
3 tbsp	sugar	4½ tbsp
½ tsp	salt	¾ tsp
2 cups	bread flour	3 cups
1½ tsp	yeast	2¼ tsp

METHOD

Put ingredients in bread pan in order suggested by your bread machine instructions. Set for sweet bread, light crust. Press Start.

Alternatively, to bake the bread in a tube pan in the oven, set bread machine for the dough stage. When ready, remove dough and punch it down. The larger loaf goes in a 9- or 10-inch tube pan. The small loaf will fit in a 6- or 7-inch tube pan or 5- or 6-cup soufflé or casserole dish. Butter the pan and turn the dough in it so all sides are buttered. Cover loosely, put in a warm spot to rise until doubled in volume. Bake in a preheated 350°F oven until golden and a skewer inserted in the bread comes out clean, 25 to 30 minutes.

LEFT Brown Sugar Pecan Bread

ANADAMA BREAD

Anadama bread is a New England hearth bread, made with cornmeal and molasses. For variety, substitute ⅔ cup whole-wheat flour for an equal amount of the bread flour.

1 lb LOAF	INGREDIENTS	1½ lb LOAF
¾ cup	water	1¼ cups
1 tbsp	vegetable oil	1½ tbsp
3 tbsp	molasses	4½ tbsp
1 tsp	salt	1½ tsp
¼ cup	cornmeal	6 tbsp
2 cups	bread flour	3 cups
1½ tsp	yeast	2¼ tsp

METHOD

Put ingredients in bread pan in order suggested by your bread machine instructions. Set for white bread, medium crust. Press Start.

Grain Breads

MULTI-GRAIN BREAD

This is a densely textured bread with the flavor of several grains. It includes enough bread flour that it rises into a small, compact loaf.

1 lb LOAF	INGREDIENTS	1½ lb LOAF
½ cup	water	¾ cup
¼ cup	milk	6 tbsp
2 tbsp	vegetable oil	3 tbsp
2 tbsp	honey	3 tbsp
1 tsp	salt	1½ tsp
¼ cup	wheat germ	6 tbsp
¼ cup	oat bran	6 tbsp
¾ cup	bread flour	1¼ cups
1 cup	whole-wheat flour	1½ cups
2 tsp	yeast	1 tbsp

METHOD

Put ingredients in bread pan in order suggested by your bread machine instructions. Set for whole-wheat bread, medium crust. Press Start.

BULGUR WHEAT BREAD

Bulgur is cracked wheat that has been parboiled. It adds fiber and crunch to whole-wheat bread.

1 lb LOAF	INGREDIENTS	1½ lb LOAF
¾ cup	buttermilk	1¼ cups
2 tbsp	vegetable oil	3 tbsp
2 tbsp	honey	3 tbsp
1 tsp	salt	1½ tsp
¼ tsp	baking soda	¼ tsp
3 tbsp	bulgur	4½ tbsp
1 tbsp	cornmeal	1½ tbsp
1 cup	bread flour	1½ cups
1 cup	whole-wheat flour	1½ cups
2 tsp	yeast	1 tbsp

METHOD

Put ingredients in bread pan in order suggested by your bread machine instructions. Set for whole-wheat bread, medium crust. Press Start.

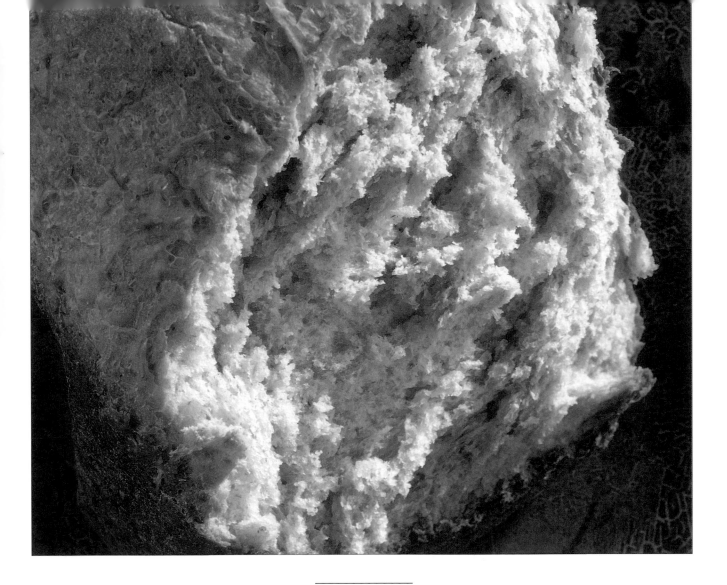

CRACKED WHEAT BUTTERMILK BREAD

This is a moist, hearty whole-wheat bread, with cracked wheat adding texture and heft. It is a good sandwich bread.

1 lb LOAF	INGREDIENTS	1½ lb LOAF
¼ cup	cracked wheat	6 tbsp
9 tbsp	buttermilk	⅞ cup
2 tbsp	butter	3 tbsp
2 tbsp	honey	3 tbsp
1 tsp	salt	1½ tsp
¼ tsp	baking soda	¼ tsp
1 cup	bread flour	1½ cups
1 cup	whole-wheat flour	1½ cups
2 tsp	yeast	1 tbsp

METHOD

Put cracked wheat in small saucepan with 1 to 2 cups water. Bring to a boil, then reduce heat to medium and let boil for 6 minutes. Remove from heat and drain thoroughly. Let wheat cool about 15 minutes.

Put cooked wheat and all other ingredients in bread pan in order suggested by your bread machine instructions. Set for whole-wheat bread, medium crust. Press Start. Check the dough after about 10 minutes of kneading. Depending on how well-drained the cracked wheat was, the bread may need a little more buttermilk or flour.

SEED BREAD

*Wheat germ, sesame seeds, and sunflower seeds add crunch
to this light whole-wheat bread.*

1 lb LOAF	INGREDIENTS	1½ lb LOAF
½ cup	buttermilk	¾ cup
⅓ cup	water	½ cup
1 tbsp	vegetable oil	1½ tbsp
1 tbsp	sugar	1½ tbsp
¼ tsp	baking soda	¼ tsp
1 tsp	salt	1½ tsp
2 tbsp	toasted wheat germ	3 tbsp
½ cup	whole-wheat flour	¾ cup
1½ cups	bread flour	2¼ cups
1½ tsp	yeast	2¼ tsp
3 tbsp	raw, shelled sunflower seeds	4½ tbsp
1 tbsp	toasted sesame seeds	1½ tbsp

METHOD

Put all ingredients except seeds in bread pan in order suggested by your bread machine instructions. Set for whole-wheat bread, medium crust. Press Start. Add seeds after first kneading or when machine beeps to add nuts.

To toast wheat germs and sesame seeds, put each in a small, ungreased skillet over medium heat. Shake the pan occasionally so seeds do not scorch. Cook until they are lightly brown. Let seeds or wheat germ cool before adding them to the dough.

MILLET BREAD

*This bread uses two forms of millet. The millet flour adds flavor, and whole
hulled millet gives it crunch. Use it for cheese on toast or for sandwiches.*

1 lb LOAF	INGREDIENTS	1½ lb LOAF
¾ cup	water	1¼ cups
1 tbsp	vegetable oil	1½ tbsp
2 tbsp	honey	3 tbsp
1 tsp	salt	1½ tsp
3 tbsp	whole hulled millet	4½ tbsp
⅓ cup	millet flour	½ cup
⅔ cup	whole-wheat flour	1 cup
1 cup	bread flour	1½ cups
2 tsp	yeast	1 tbsp

METHOD

Put ingredients in bread pan in order suggested by your bread machine instructions. Set for whole-wheat bread, medium crust. Press Start.

LEFT Seed Bread

MAPLE-PECAN BREAKFAST BREAD

This multi-grain bread is sweetened with maple syrup, but it is still not a sweet bread. Flavor also comes from pecans, which are added at the beginning and ground up by the kneading action. Bulgur wheat, softened slightly by boiling water, also adds texture.

1 lb LOAF	INGREDIENTS	1½ lb LOAF
¼ cup	bulgur wheat	6 tbsp
¼ cup	boiling water	6 tbsp
½ cup	milk	¾ cup
2 tbsp	butter	3 tbsp
3 tbsp	maple syrup	4½ tbsp
1 tsp	salt	1½ tsp
¼ cup	chopped pecans	6 tbsp
¼ cup	oat bran	6 tbsp
¾ cup	whole-wheat flour	1¼ cups
1 cup	bread flour	1½ cups
1½ tsp	yeast	2¼ tsp

METHOD

Put bulgur in bread pan. Pour boiling water over it and stir. Let cool 15 minutes. Put remaining ingredients in bread pan in order suggested by your bread machine instructions. Set for whole-wheat bread, medium crust. Press Start.

PRUNE WALNUT BRAN BREAD

This is a delicious bread, made moist and slightly sweet by prunes, and fortified with bran cereal. Even prune-haters like this bread, as long as they don't know prunes are the secret ingredient. The walnuts are added at the beginning, so they are ground up more finely than usual, adding more flavor than crunch.

1 lb LOAF	INGREDIENTS	1½ lb LOAF
⅔ cup	water	1 cup
3 tbsp	powdered milk	4½ tbsp
½ cup	chopped pitted prunes	¾ cup
1 tbsp	vegetable oil	1½ tbsp
1 tbsp	molasses	1½ tbsp
1 tsp	salt	1½ tsp
¼ cup	chopped walnuts	6 tbsp
½ cup	bran flakes (cereal)	¾ cup
1 cup	whole-wheat flour	1½ cups
1 cup	bread flour	1½ cups
1½ tsp	yeast	2¼ tsp

METHOD

Put ingredients in bread pan in order suggested by your bread machine instructions. Set for whole-wheat bread, medium crust. Press Start.

COCONUT BANANA BRAN BREAD

This is a dense, hearty bread, only slightly sweet, but fragrant with tropical flavors. It makes excellent toast, but don't limit yourself to butter – spread it with cream cheese or peanut butter. Use a bran cereal such as All-Bran, not bran flakes.

1 lb LOAF	INGREDIENTS	1½ lb LOAF
1	egg	1
¼ cup	milk	½ cup
⅓ cup	mashed ripe banana	½ cup
2 tbsp	butter	3 tbsp
2 tbsp	honey	3 tbsp
¼ cup	flaked coconut	6 tbsp
½ tsp	salt	¾ tsp
⅓ cup	bran cereal	½ cup
1 cup	whole-wheat flour	1½ cups
1 cup	bread flour	1½ cups
1½ tsp	yeast	2¼ tsp

METHOD

Put ingredients in bread pan in order suggested by your bread machine instructions. Set for whole-wheat bread, medium crust. Press Start.

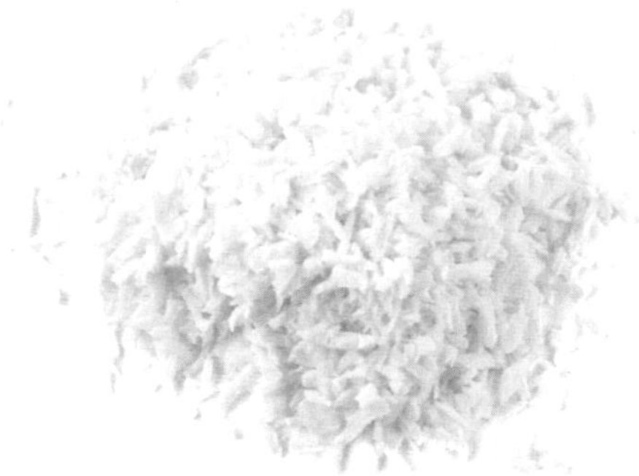

BRAN CEREAL BREAD

This is a dense but moist bread, high in fiber provided by bran cereal (not flakes) such as All-Bran. It makes good bread for toast or sandwiches.

1 lb LOAF	INGREDIENTS	1½ lb LOAF
⅞ cup	milk	1⅓ cups
1 tbsp	vegetable oil	1½ tbsp
1 tbsp	sugar	1½ tbsp
1 tsp	salt	1½ tsp
⅓ cup	bran cereal	½ cup
¾ cup	whole-wheat flour	1¼ cups
1 cup	bread flour	1½ cups
1½ tsp	yeast	2¼ tsp

METHOD

Put ingredients in bread pan in order suggested by your bread machine instructions. Set for whole-wheat bread, medium crust. Press Start.

RIGHT Coconut Banana Bran Bread

HONEY ORANGE MULTI-GRAIN BREAD

This bread, perfect for breakfast, is dense with a soft texture, moist and flavorful. Millet and bulgur wheat add a little crunch.

1 lb LOAF	INGREDIENTS	1½ lb LOAF
⅓ cup	water	½ cup
½ cup	buttermilk	¾ cup
1 tbsp	vegetable oil	1½ tbsp
2 tbsp	honey	3 tbsp
1 tbsp	grated orange rind	1½ tbsp
1 tsp	salt	1½ tsp
1 tbsp	bulgur wheat	1½ tbsp
1 tbsp	whole hulled wheat	1½ tbsp
¼ cup	soy flour	6 tbsp
¼ cup	amaranth flour	6 tbsp
⅔ cup	whole-wheat flour	1 cup
1⅓ cups	bread flour	2 cups
2 tsp	yeast	1 tbsp

METHOD

Put ingredients in bread pan in order suggested by your bread machine instructions. Set for whole-wheat bread, medium crust. Press Start.

WHEAT GERM YOGURT BREAD

This healthy bread has a dense but soft texture. It is good for toast or sandwiches.

1 lb LOAF	INGREDIENTS	1½ lb LOAF
½ cup	plain yogurt	¾ cup
¼ cup	water	6 tbsp
1 tbsp	vegetable oil	1½ tbsp
2 tbsp	honey	3 tbsp
1 tsp	salt	1½ tsp
3 tbsp	powdered milk	4½ tbsp
¼ cup	toasted wheat germ	6 tbsp
1 cup	bread flour	1½ cups
1 cup	whole-wheat flour	1½ cups
2 tsp	yeast	1 tbsp

METHOD

Put ingredients in bread pan in order suggested by your bread machine instructions. Set for whole-wheat bread, medium crust. Press Start.

To toast wheat germ, put it in a small dry skillet over medium heat. Cook, shaking occasionally so germ doesn't scorch, until lightly browned. Let wheat germ cool before adding it to the dough.

SUNSHINE BREAD

*This is a light, whole-wheat bread from California, full of dates and
sunflower seeds. It makes good toast and vegetarian-type sandwiches
of avocado or cream cheese.*

1 lb LOAF	INGREDIENTS	1½ lb LOAF
½ cup	sour cream	¾ cup
¼ cup	water	6 tbsp
2 tbsp	butter	3 tbsp
2 tbsp	honey	3 tbsp
½ tsp	salt	¾ tsp
2 tbsp	oat bran	3 tbsp
½ cup	whole-wheat flour	¾ cup
1½ cups	bread flour	2¼ cups
1½ tsp	yeast	2¼ tsp
3 tbsp	sunflower seeds	4½ tbsp
¼ cup	chopped dates	6 tbsp

METHOD

Put all ingredients except sunflower seeds and dates in
bread pan in order suggested by your bread machine
instructions. Set for whole-wheat bread, medium crust.
Press Start. Add seeds and dates at the beeper or after
first kneading.

Apple Bran Bread

This breakfast bread, fragrant with apple and cinnamon and enriched with wheat germ and bran cereal, makes excellent toast. As the water content of apples varies, you may need to add a small amount of water or flour. However, check the dough late in the kneading stage, as the bran flakes will absorb some liquid.

1 lb LOAF	INGREDIENTS	1½ lb LOAF
⅓ cup	peeled, grated apple	½ cup
½ cup	water	¾ cup
2 tbsp	butter	3 tbsp
2 tbsp	honey	3 tbsp
3 tbsp	powdered milk	4½ tbsp
1 tsp	salt	1½ tsp
1 tsp	cinnamon	1½ tsp
½ cup	bran flakes (cereal)	¾ cup
2 tbsp	toasted wheat germ	3 tbsp
1 cup	whole-wheat flour	1½ cups
¾ cup	bread flour	1¼ cups
1½ tsp	yeast	2¼ tsp

METHOD

Put ingredients in bread pan in order suggested by your bread machine instructions. Set for whole-wheat bread, medium crust. Press Start.

To toast wheat germ, put it in a small, dry skillet. Cook over medium heat until browned. Shake and stir frequently to keep wheat germ from scorching. Let it cool before adding to bread pan.

Fruit, Vegetable, Nut and Cheese Breads

Date Granola Bread
49

Sweet Potato Bread
49

Zucchini Bread
50

Cottage Cheese Dill Bread
50

Chili Cheese Bread
52

Basil Tomato Parmesan Bread
53

Pumpkin Pecan Bread
54

Cherry Hazelnut Bread
55

Olive Cheese Bread
56

Oatmeal Walnut Bread
56

Apple Sauce Hazelnut Bread
58

Ricotta Walnut Herb Bread
58

Tropical Pineapple Bread
59

Cinnamon Raisin Bread
60

Laura's Ginger Applesauce Bread
60

Mango Macadamia Nut Bread
61

Trail Mix Bread
62

Apricot Graham Bread
62

Pear Bread
64

Cranberry Orange Bread
65

Buttermilk Fruit Bread
66

Sweet Red Pepper Sage Bread
67

California Almond Fig Bread
68

Almond Poppyseed Bread
68

DATE GRANOLA BREAD

The variety of granolas available is tremendous. Different types can entirely change the character of the bread. Other than additions like dried fruits and nuts, the biggest difference is in sweetness. This bread, served untoasted with butter, was a favorite with the friends who tried many of my experiments.

1 lb LOAF	INGREDIENTS	1½ lb LOAF
½ cup	water	¾ cup
¼ cup	milk	6 tbsp
1 tbsp	vegetable oil	1½ tbsp
1 tbsp	honey	1½ tbsp
½ tsp	cinnamon	¾ tsp
1 tsp	salt	1½ tsp
½ cup	granola	¾ cup
1¼ cups	bread flour	1⅞ cups
½ cup	whole-wheat flour	¾ cup
1½ tsp	yeast	2¼ tsp
⅓ cup	chopped dates	½ cup

METHOD

Put all ingredients except dates in bread pan in order suggested by your bread machine instructions. Set for whole-wheat bread, medium crust. Press Start. Add dates after first kneading or when machine beeps to add fruit.

This recipe is based on a basic, not-too-sweet granola. You can adjust the amount of honey in the recipe if you're starting with a particularly sweet granola, substitute other fruit, or add nuts. Omit the cinnamon if the granola is already spiced.

SWEET POTATO BREAD

Sweet potato bread has its roots in the southern United States. It has a delicate flavor and pale orange color, but is not a sweet bread. Serve it as an accompaniment to soup or salad, or top it with melted cheese.

1 lb LOAF	INGREDIENTS	1½ lb LOAF
⅔ cup	cooked, mashed sweet potatoes	1 cup
6 tbsp	milk	9 tbsp
2 tbsp	butter	3 tbsp
2 tbsp	sugar	3 tbsp
1 tsp	salt	1½ tsp
2 cups	bread flour	3 cups
2 tsp	yeast	1 tbsp

METHOD

Put ingredients in bread pan in order suggested by your bread machine instructions. Set for whole-wheat bread, medium crust.

You may use canned sweet potatoes for this recipe, but only if there is no sugar or syrup added. Otherwise, bake or boil sweet potatoes and mash them without any additions. The amount of milk needed may vary slightly depending on the water content of the sweet potatoes.

ZUCCHINI BREAD

This is a medium-weight whole-wheat bread. Cottage cheese lightens it, bulgur wheat adds crunch, and zucchini adds subtle flavor. It makes excellent toast and is also good for sandwiches. The amount of water needed may vary, depending on the water content of the cottage cheese, so check the dough during kneading.

1 lb LOAF	INGREDIENTS	1½ lb LOAF
½ cup	cottage cheese	¾ cup
¼ cup	water	6 tbsp
½ cup	grated raw zucchini	¾ cup
2 tbsp	butter	3 tbsp
1 tbsp	sugar	1½ tbsp
1 tsp	salt	1½ tsp
3 tbsp	bulgur wheat	4½ tbsp
⅔ cup	whole-wheat flour	1 cup
1⅓ cups	bread flour	2 cups
1½ tsp	yeast	2¼ tsp

METHOD

Put ingredients in bread pan in order suggested by your bread machine instructions. Set for whole wheat-bread, medium crust. Press Start.

COTTAGE CHEESE DILL BREAD

Cottage cheese gives this bread a feathery light texture. Try it in a sandwich. The amount of water needed may vary slightly, depending on the liquid content of the cottage cheese.

1 lb LOAF	INGREDIENTS	1½ lb LOAF
⅔ cup	cottage cheese	1 cup
1	egg	1 egg + 1 yolk
2½ tbsp	water	4 tbsp
1 tbsp	butter	1½ tbsp
1 tbsp	honey	1½ tbsp
½ tsp	salt	¾ tsp
1½ cups	bread flour	2¼ cups
½ cup	whole-wheat flour	¾ cup
2 tsp	dried dill	1 tbsp
1½ tsp	yeast	2¼ tsp

METHOD

Put ingredients in bread pan in order suggested by your bread machine instructions. Set for whole-wheat bread, medium crust. Press Start.

RIGHT Zucchini Bread

CHILI CHEESE BREAD

This is a very flavorful bread, with the complementary tastes of Cheddar cheese and green chilies. If using fresh chilies, choose Anaheims, green New Mexico chilies, or poblanos. You may add a jalapeno or two serrano chilies for extra heat. A note at the bottom of this recipe tells how to roast your own chilies, but you can substitute canned green chilies with a small loss of flavor. This is a hearty bread that goes well with soups, stews, and salads.

1 lb LOAF	INGREDIENTS	1½ lb LOAF
2	roasted and chopped chilies	3
1	egg	1
⅓ cup	milk	9 tbsp
⅔ cup	grated sharp Cheddar cheese	1 cup
2 tbsp	butter	3 tbsp
1 tsp	sugar	1½ tsp
1 tsp	salt	1½ tsp
2 cups	bread flour	3 cups
1½ tsp	yeast	2¼ tsp

METHOD

Put ingredients in bread pan in order suggested by your bread machine instructions. Set for white bread, medium crust. Press Start.

To roast chilies: set oven to broil. Cut chilies in half lengthwise (poblanos should be cut in three or four lengthwise pieces). Remove stems and seeds, taking care to avoid handling the seeds or inner veins. Place skin side up on foil or broiler pan 4 to 6 inches under broiler. Broil until the skin is blistered and mostly brown or black, but don't let the flesh burn. Don't expect the skin to cook uniformly. Remove chilies from broiler and place in bag or foil envelope and close. Let the chilies steam in the foil or bag for about 10 minutes. Remove chilies from bag. Peel and discard skin. Chop chilies.

Basil Tomato Parmesan Bread

This is a moist and savory bread, seasoned with basil, Parmesan cheese, and sun-dried tomatoes. Serve it with sweet butter, or use it for sandwiches. You can add the tomatoes at the beginning or after the initial kneading. If you add the tomatoes at the same time as the other ingredients, the bread will be a deep red-orange with very few bits of tomato.

1 lb LOAF	INGREDIENTS	1½ lb LOAF
½ cup	water	¾ cup
¼ cup	milk	6 tbsp
2 tbsp	olive oil	3 tbsp
1 tsp	sugar	1½ tsp
1 tsp	salt	1½ tsp
2 tsp	dried basil	3 tsp
⅓ cup	grated Parmesan cheese	½ cup
2 cups	bread flour	3 cups
2 tsp	yeast	1 tbsp
¼ cup	chopped sun-dried tomatoes	6 tbsp

METHOD

Add all ingredients except tomatoes in the order suggested by bread machine instructions. Set machine for white bread, medium crust. Press Start.

If tomatoes are oil-packed, blot them dry. (Tomato oil may be used instead of all or part of the olive oil in the recipe.) Chop tomatoes or cut with kitchen scissors. Add them to the dough after the first kneading, or when the beeper indicates it is time to add fruit.

PUMPKIN PECAN BREAD

*This is not the traditional sweet, dense, baking powder pumpkin bread, but
a light and slightly sweet yeast bread that is flavored with pumpkin, pecans,
and spices. Eat it warm with butter or make turkey sandwiches with it.*

1 lb LOAF	INGREDIENTS	1½ lb LOAF
⅓ cup	milk	½ cup
¾ cup	puréed pumpkin	1¼ cups
2 tbsp	butter	3 tbsp
3 tbsp	sugar	4½ tbsp
½ tsp	salt	¾ tsp
1 tsp	cinnamon	1½ tsp
½ tsp	ground ginger	¾ tsp
¼ tsp	ground cloves	¼ tsp
½ cup	chopped pecans	¾ cup
2 cups	bread flour	3 cups
2 tsp	yeast	1 tbsp

METHOD

Put ingredients in bread pan in order suggested by your
bread machine instructions. Set for white bread, light
crust. Press Start.

The amount of milk needed may vary slightly, depending
on the water content of the pumpkin. Be sure you are
using pure pumpkin, not pumpkin pie filling.

CHERRY HAZELNUT BREAD

This is a light whole-wheat bread, made special by the addition of tart dried cherries and toasted hazelnuts. It is not a sweet bread, so it goes with meals.

1 lb LOAF	INGREDIENTS	1½ lb LOAF
½ cup	milk	⅞ cup
1	egg	1
2 tbsp	butter	3 tbsp
2 tbsp	sugar	3 tbsp
½ tsp	salt	¾ tsp
1½ cups	bread flour	2¼ cups
½ cup	whole-wheat flour	¾ cup
1½ tsp	yeast	2¼ tsp
¼ cup	dried cherries	6 tbsp
3 tbsp	chopped toasted hazelnuts	4½ tbsp

METHOD

Put all ingredients except cherries and hazelnuts in bread pan in order suggested by your bread machine instructions. Set for whole-wheat bread, medium crust. Press Start. Add cherries and hazelnuts after the first kneading, or when the machine signals to add fruit.

Note: To toast shelled hazelnuts, spread them in a single layer on an ungreased baking sheet. Bake them in a 350°F oven for 10 minutes, stirring two or three times. Allow the nuts to cool, wrap them in a coarse towel, and rub them together to remove the papery membrane.

Olive Cheese Bread

This is an assertive bread, flavored with green olives, feta cheese, sun-dried tomatoes, and thyme. Serve it with pasta, homemade tomato soup, antipasto, or salad. It can be baked in the bread machine, or shaped into a round loaf and baked in the oven.

1 lb LOAF	INGREDIENTS	1½ lb LOAF
⅔ cup	water	1 cup
2 tbsp	olive oil	3 tbsp
1 tbsp	sugar	1½ tbsp
½ tsp	dried thyme	¾ tsp
1 tsp	salt	1½ tsp
2 cups	bread flour	3 cups
1½ tsp	yeast	2¼ tsp
⅓ cup	crumbled feta cheese	½ cup
¼ cup	coarsely chopped green olives	6 tbsp
2 tbsp	chopped sun-dried tomatoes	3 tbsp
2 tbsp	bread flour	3 tbsp

METHOD

Put first seven ingredients in bread pan in order suggested by your bread machine instructions. Set for white bread, medium crust. Press Start. Toss remaining ingredients with flour, then add them to the dough after first kneading or at the beeper.

To bake in the oven, set the bread machine for dough stage. When dough is ready, remove and punch down. Shape into a round loaf. Put on a baking sheet that has been sprinkled with cornmeal. Cover loosely and put in a warm place to rise until doubled in volume. Brush the surface with a glaze of 1 egg mixed with 1 tbsp water, and bake in a preheated 350°F oven until golden, about 25 minutes.

Oatmeal Walnut Bread

Old-fashioned rolled oats add a nice texture to this breakfast bread.

1 lb LOAF	INGREDIENTS	1½ lb LOAF
½ cup	milk	¾ cup
¼ cup	water	6 tbsp
1 tbsp	butter	1½ tbsp
2 tbsp	honey	3 tbsp
1 tsp	salt	1½ tsp
1¾ cups	bread flour	2⅔ cups
½ cup	rolled oats	¾ cup
½ cup	chopped walnuts	¾ cup
1½ tsp	yeast	2¼ tsp

METHOD

Put ingredients in bread pan in order suggested by your bread machine instructions. Set for white bread, medium crust. Press Start.

RIGHT Olive Cheese Bread

Applesauce Hazelnut Bread

*This apple-flavored bread is only slightly sweet, but fragrant with spice.
Oatmeal and hazelnuts give it a nice texture. It is best as a breakfast bread.*

1 lb LOAF	INGREDIENTS	1½ lb LOAF
½ cup	old-fashioned rolled oats	¾ cup
⅓ cup	boiling water	½ cup
⅓ cup	unsweetened applesauce	½ cup
¼ cup	water	90 ml (3 fl oz)
1 tbsp	vegetable oil	1½ tbsp
1 tbsp	honey	1½ tbsp
½ tsp	cinnamon	¾ tsp
¼ tsp	allspice	½ tsp
2 tbsp	powdered milk	3 tbsp
½ tsp	salt	¾ tsp
1¾ cups	bread flour	2½ cups
1½ tsp	yeast	2¼ tsp
40 g (1½ oz)	chopped toasted hazelnuts	60 g (2¼ oz)

METHOD

Put oatmeal in bread pan. Pour boiling water over oatmeal. Stir and let sit 15 minutes. Add remaining ingredients, except hazelnuts, in order suggested by your bread machine instructions. Set for white bread, medium crust. Press Start. Add hazelnuts after first kneading or at beeper.

The applesauce should be thick. If it is runny, simmer it in a small saucepan to evaporate excess water. Measure the applesauce after cooking, since water may account for nearly half the volume of some store-bought applesauce. Also check the dough after five minutes of kneading and add water or flour if needed. Omit the honey if the applesauce is pre-sweetened.

Ricotta Walnut Herb Bread

Try this bread with meatloaf sandwiches, pasta, light soups, and salads.

1 lb LOAF	INGREDIENTS	1½ lb LOAF
2 tbsp	olive oil	3 tbsp
1 tsp	dried basil	1½ tsp
⅔ cup	ricotta cheese	1 cup
1	egg	1 egg + 1 yolk
3 tbsp	milk	4½ tbsp
2 tsp	sugar	1 tbsp
1 tsp	salt	1½ tsp
2 cups	bread flour	3 cups
1½ tsp	yeast	2¼ tsp
¼ cup	chopped walnuts	6 tbsp

METHOD

Heat oil in a skillet. Add basil. Cook for 1 minute over low heat. Remove from heat and let it cool.

Drain off any watery liquid from the ricotta cheese.

Put cooled basil oil, drained ricotta, and all remaining ingredients except walnuts in bread pan in order suggested by your bread machine instructions. Set for white bread, medium crust. Press Start. Add the walnuts at the beeper or after the first kneading.

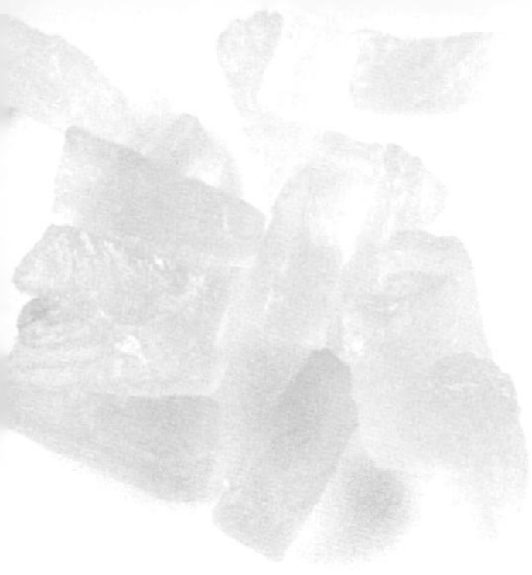

TROPICAL PINEAPPLE BREAD

Candied pineapple sweetens this bread, which is also flavored with coconut, nutmeg, and ginger. It is delicious toasted and spread with cream cheese.

1 lb LOAF	INGREDIENTS	1½ lb LOAF
½ cup	water	¾ cup
¼ cup	milk	6 tbsp
2 tbsp	butter	3 tbsp
2 tbsp	honey	3 tbsp
¼ tsp	ground ginger	½ tsp
¼ tsp	nutmeg	½ tsp
½ tsp	salt	¾ tsp
½ cup	whole-wheat flour	¾ cup
1½ cups	bread flour	2¼ cups
1½ tsp	yeast	2¼ tsp
⅓ cup	diced sugared pineapple	½ cup
¼ cup	grated coconut	6 tbsp
¼ cup	chopped macadamia nuts	6 tbsp

METHOD

Put all but last three ingredients in bread pan in order suggested by your bread machine instructions. Add about half the pineapple, which will be cut into bits by the kneading. Set for white bread, medium crust. Press Start. Add remaining pineapple, coconut, and nuts at beeper or after first kneading.

CINNAMON RAISIN BREAD

This is a light, slightly sweet whole-wheat bread. It is good for toast, and delicious with apple or pumpkin butter.

1 lb LOAF	INGREDIENTS	1½ lb LOAF
½ cup	water	¾ cup
¼ cup	milk	6 tbsp
2 tbsp	butter	3 tbsp
3 tbsp	brown sugar	4½ tbsp
½ tsp	salt	¾ tsp
2 tsp	cinnamon	1 tbsp
1½ cups	bread flour	2¼ cups
½ cup	whole-wheat flour	¾ cup
2 tsp	yeast	1 tbsp
⅓ cup	raisins	½ cup

METHOD

Put all ingredients except raisins in bread pan in order suggested by your bread machine instructions. Set for whole-wheat bread, medium crust. Press Start. Add raisins after the first kneading, or when the machine signals that it is time to add fruit.

If you want whole raisins, add them after the first kneading. Add them at the beginning if you want a darker color and an overall sweeter, raisiny taste. If your raisins are so dry that you plump them up in hot water, blot every bit of water off them before adding them. Wet raisins will alter the flour/liquid balance.

LAURA'S GINGER APPLESAUCE BREAD

The flavor of ginger and apples is just right in this bread, tasty but not overwhelming. Graham flour gives it good texture.

1 lb LOAF	INGREDIENTS	1½ lb LOAF
⅓ cup	water	½ cup
½ cup	unsweetened applesauce	¾ cup
2 tbsp	powdered milk	3 tbsp
1 tbsp	butter	1½ tbsp
2 tbsp	molasses	3 tbsp
1 tsp	ground ginger	1½ tsp
½ tsp	salt	¾ tsp
1 cup	bread flour	1½ cups
1 cup	graham flour	1½ cups
1½ tsp	yeast	2¼ tsp

METHOD

Put ingredients in bread pan in order suggested by your bread machine instructions. Set for whole-wheat bread, medium crust. Press Start.

The amount of water needed will depend on the water content of the applesauce. If the applesauce is runny, simmer it on the stovetop to evaporate excess water. Check the dough during kneading to see if the amount of flour or water needs to be adjusted.

MANGO MACADAMIA NUT BREAD

With its tropical flavor, this bread goes well with a fruited chicken salad sandwich.

1 lb LOAF	INGREDIENTS	1½ lb LOAF
⅓ cup	old-fashioned rolled oats	½ cup
¼ cup	boiling water	6 tbsp
½ cup	puréed mango	¾ cup
¼ cup	milk	6 tbsp
1 tbsp	butter	1½ tbsp
2 tsp	sugar	1 tbsp
½ tsp	salt	¾ tsp
¼ tsp	ground ginger	½ tsp
¼ tsp	nutmeg	½ tsp
1¾ cups	bread flour	2⅔ cups
2 tsp	yeast	1 tbsp
¼ cup	chopped macadamia nuts	6 tbsp

METHOD

Put the oats in bread machine pan and pour the boiling water over them. Stir so all the oats are wet. Let sit at least 15 minutes. Add all the remaining ingredients except the nuts. Set for white bread, medium crust. Press Start. Check the dough after about 10 minutes. Depending on the water content of the mango, the dough may need a little more milk or flour. Add the nuts after the first kneading or when the machine signals to add fruit or nuts.

TRAIL MIX BREAD

Trail mix is a kitchen-sink sort of concoction made up of any kind of dried fruit, seeds, or nuts, from the ordinary to the exotic, and may be sweetened with bits of coconut, or other goodies. Likewise, Trail Mix Bread is a kitchen-sink sort of bread.

1 lb LOAF	INGREDIENTS	1½ lb LOAF
½ cup	water	¾ cup
¼ cup	milk	6 tbsp
2 tbsp	vegetable oil	3 tbsp
2 tbsp	honey	3 tbsp
1 tsp	salt	1½ tsp
1⅓ cups	bread flour	2 cups
⅔ cup	whole-wheat flour	1 cup
1½ tsp	yeast	2¼ tsp
½ cup	trail mix	¾ cup

METHOD

Put all ingredients except trail mix in bread pan in order suggested by your bread machine instructions. Set for whole-wheat bread, medium crust. Press Start. Add trail mix at the beeper or after first kneading.

If the only trail mix you can find is a mix of raisins and sunflower seeds, doctor it with dates, dried apricots, dried cherries, pecans, or cashews. Coarsely chop whole nuts such as almonds. Avoid using chocolate in the trail mix as it tends to burn in a bread machine.

APRICOT GRAHAM BREAD

Dried apricots and molasses give this bread a hint of sweetness, while the graham flour gives it a slightly chewy texture. It's a delicious breakfast bread that also goes well with chicken or cream cheese sandwiches.

1 lb LOAF	INGREDIENTS	1½ lb LOAF
⅔ cup	water	1 cup
1 tbsp	vegetable oil	1½ tbsp
2 tbsp	molasses	3 tbsp
⅓ cup	coarsely chopped dried apricots	½ cup
2 tbsp	powdered milk	3 tbsp
½ tsp	salt	¾ tsp
1 cup	bread flour	1½ cups
1 cup	graham flour	1½ cups
1½ tsp	yeast	2¼ tsp

METHOD

Put ingredients in bread pan in order suggested by your bread machine instructions. Set for whole-wheat bread, medium crust. Press Start.

RIGHT Trail Mix Bread

PEAR BREAD

This is based on a bread made in the French countryside amid pear orchards. It has a delicate, sweet flavor of pears. It is a nice tea or breakfast bread, or can be used in mildly flavored sandwiches such as cream cheese and cucumber.

1 lb LOAF	INGREDIENTS	1½ lb LOAF
½ cup	pear purée	¾ cup
about 3 tbsp	pear liquid or water	4–5 tbsp
2 tsp	honey	1 tbsp
2 tbsp	butter	3 tbsp
½ tsp	salt	¼ tsp
½ tsp	ground ginger	¼ tsp
½ tsp	nutmeg	¼ tsp
2 cups	bread flour	3 cups
1½ tsp	yeast	2¼ tsp

METHOD

Make the pear purée by peeling and coring 3 pears for the smaller recipe, 4 or 5 pears for the larger one. Cut each pear in several pieces and put in a small saucepan with 1 or 2 tbsp water. Start cooking over very low heat. The pears will quickly start releasing their own juices, and no more water will be needed. Increase to medium heat. Cook the pears until they are very soft, about 10 minutes. Then drain off as much liquid as you can, saving the liquid. Put the pears in a blender or food processor and purée.

Measure out the required amount of purée. Put it and all other ingredients except pear liquid in bread pan in order suggested by your bread machine instructions. The amount of liquid needed for the bread will depend on the liquid in the purée, so you'll need to watch the dough for the first few minutes, adding pear liquid (or plain water) until it reaches the proper consistency – neither stiff nor too soft. Set for white bread, medium crust. Press Start. Once you have added the liquid, the bread does not need any further attention until it is baked.

CRANBERRY ORANGE BREAD

This bread is flavored with cranberries and orange peel, but don't save it only for the holidays. It is slightly sweet, but is not sweet enough to be a dessert bread. Use it for toast or sandwiches of turkey or pork.

1 lb LOAF	INGREDIENTS	1½ lb LOAF
½ cup	water	¾ cup
2 tbsp	butter	3 tbsp
3 tbsp	sugar	4½ tbsp
½ tsp	salt	¾ tsp
2 tsp	grated orange peel	1 tbsp
½ tsp	nutmeg	¾ tsp
⅔ cup	cranberries	1 cup
½ cup	whole-wheat flour	¾ cup
1½ cups	bread flour	2¼ cups
2 tsp	yeast	1 tbsp

METHOD

Put ingredients in bread pan in order suggested by your bread machine instructions. Set for white bread, medium crust. Press Start.

You may use fresh or frozen cranberries, but allow frozen cranberries to thaw before adding them to the dough. If you add whole cranberries at the same time as the other ingredients, the kneading action of the bread machine will chop them to the right size. Although the dough may initially seem dry, it will gain some liquid from the cranberries.

BUTTERMILK FRUIT BREAD

This is a light whole-wheat buttermilk bread with dried fruit and a pinch of cinnamon for flavor. Use any combination of dried fruit, including peaches, apricots, cherries, raisins, and figs.

1 lb LOAF	INGREDIENTS	1½ lb LOAF
½ cup	buttermilk	⅞ cup
1	egg	1
2 tbsp	butter	3 tbsp
2 tbsp	sugar	3 tbsp
½ tsp	salt	¾ tsp
½ tsp	baking soda	½ tsp
½ tsp	cinnamon	¾ tsp
1½ cups	bread flour	2¼ cups
½ cup	whole-wheat flour	¾ cup
1½ tsp	yeast	2¼ tsp
⅓ cup	coarsely chopped dried fruit	½ cup

METHOD

Put all ingredients except fruit in bread pan in order suggested by your bread machine instructions. Set for whole-wheat bread, medium crust. Press Start. Add fruit after the first kneading or when the machine beeps that it's time to add fruit.

Sweet Red Pepper Sage Bread

Made with semolina flour, this is a very light bread. The sage, toasted sesame seeds, and roasted sweet red bell peppers make it very flavorful.

1 lb LOAF	INGREDIENTS	1½ lb LOAF
½ cup	milk	¾ cup
⅓ cup	chopped, roasted sweet red peppers	½ cup
2 tbsp	olive oil	3 tbsp
1 tbsp	sugar	1½ tbsp
3 tbsp	toasted sesame seeds	4½ tbsp
1 tsp	salt	1½ tsp
½ tsp	dried sage	¾ tsp
1⅓ cups	bread flour	2 cups
⅔ cup	semolina flour	1 cup
1½ tsp	yeast	2¼ tsp

METHOD

Put ingredients in bread pan in order suggested by your bread machine instructions. Set for white bread, medium crust. Press Start

To toast sesame seeds: put seeds in a small, dry skillet over medium heat. Stir or shake the pan frequently to stop seeds from scorching. Let seeds cool before using.

To roast sweet red bell peppers: cut each pepper into 3 or 4 nearly flat pieces. Place on broiler pan or doubled sheet of aluminum foil. Cook under the broiler until skin turns black and blisters. The pieces won't cook evenly; remove each piece when it is done. As you remove each piece, put it in a bag or foil envelope to steam for 10 minutes, then peel off skin.

If you add the peppers at the beginning of the kneading, in combination with yellow semolina flour they will turn the bread orange. They will also release more moisture into the bread. If you add the peppers late in the kneading, you may need to add another tablespoon of milk. You may use bottled roasted red peppers or roast your own.

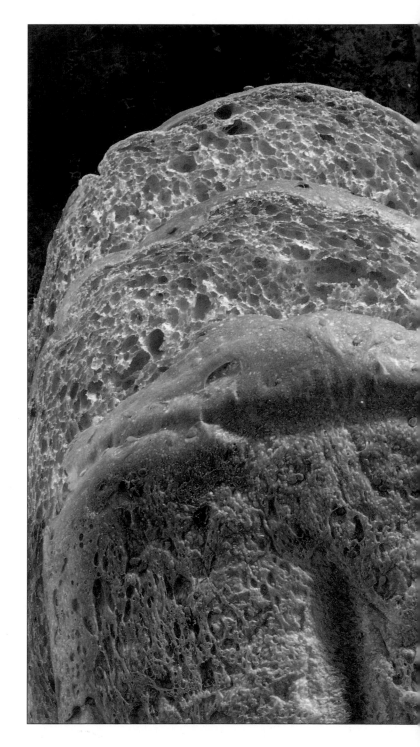

CALIFORNIA ALMOND FIG BREAD

*The additions to this yogurt bread – almonds and figs – come from
California's Central Valley. It is not a sweet bread, although the figs give
it a hint of sweetness.*

1 lb LOAF	INGREDIENTS	1½ lb LOAF
½ cup	plain yogurt	¾ cup
¼ cup	water	6 tbsp
1 tbsp	vegetable oil	1½ tbsp
2 tbsp	honey	3 tbsp
½ tsp	salt	¾ tsp
3 tbsp	oat bran	4½ tbsp
2 cups	bread flour	3 cups
1½ tsp	yeast	2¼ tsp
⅓ cup	coarsely chopped figs	½ cup
3 tbsp	slivered blanched almonds	4½ tbsp

METHOD

Put all ingredients except figs and almonds in bread pan
in order suggested by your bread machine instructions.
Set for white bread, medium crust. Press Start. Add figs
and almonds after the first kneading, or when the
machine signals that it is time to add fruit.

ALMOND POPPYSEED BREAD

*This is a light, barely sweet bread, with oatmeal adding texture. It is a good bread
for breakfast or a snack, and not at all like those gummy, overly sweet muffins.*

1 lb LOAF	INGREDIENTS	1½ lb LOAF
1	egg	1
½ cup	milk	⅞ cup
2 tbsp	butter	3 tbsp
2 tbsp	sugar	3 tbsp
1 tsp	almond extract	1½ tsp
2 tbsp	poppy seeds	3 tbsp
½ tsp	salt	¾ tsp
⅓ cup	old-fashioned rolled oats	½ cup
1¾ cups	bread flour	2⅔ cups
1½ tsp	yeast	2¼ tsp
¼ cup	slivered almonds	6 tbsp

METHOD

Put all ingredients except almonds in bread pan in order
suggested by your bread machine instructions. Set for
white bread, medium crust. Press Start. Add almonds at
the beeper or after the first kneading.

Oven-Baked Breads, Rolls, Breadsticks, and Bagels

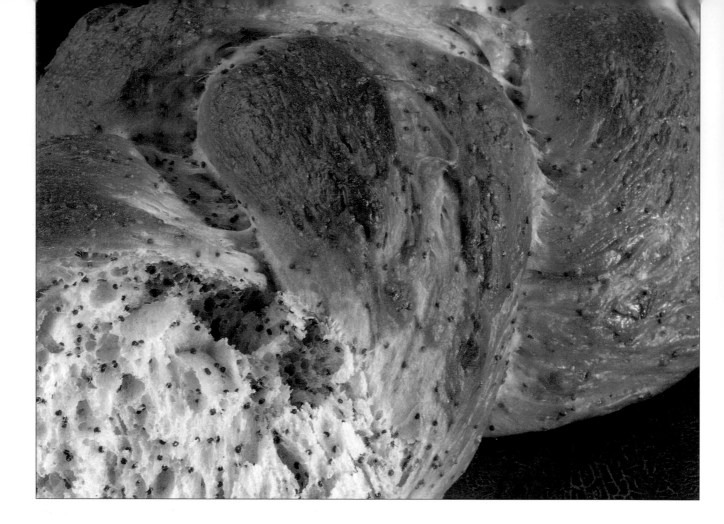

LEMON POPPYSEED BRAID

*Slightly sweet, flavored with lemon, and full of poppy seeds, this braided
bread makes an impressive appearance at brunch or tea.*

1 lb LOAF	INGREDIENTS	1½ lb LOAF
1	egg	1 egg + 1 yolk
½ cup	lemon yogurt	¾ cup
3 tbsp	butter	4½ tbsp
3 tbsp	sugar	4½ tbsp
3 tbsp	poppy seeds	4½ tbsp
2 tsp	grated lemon peel	1 tbsp
1 tsp	salt	1½ tsp
2 cups	bread flour	3 cups
1½ tsp	yeast	2¼ tsp

GLAZE

1 egg white beaten with 2 tsp water

METHOD

Put all dough ingredients in bread machine pan. Set for
white or sweet bread, dough stage. Press Start.

When dough is ready, remove from pan and punch
down. Cut into three equal pieces. Let it rest 5 minutes.
Butter a baking sheet. Roll each piece of dough into a
rope, about 14 inches for smaller loaf, 18 to 20 inches
for larger loaf. Braid three ropes together and tuck ends
under. Cover dough and put in a warm place to rise
until doubled, 45 minutes to 1 hour.

Brush dough with egg-water wash. Bake bread in a
preheated 350°F oven until golden, 25 to 30 minutes.

CROISSANTS

This is a much simplified version of the flaky layered croissant that requires so much time and patience to make. It is very buttery, but the butter is kneaded into the dough with the other ingredients instead of being folded in afterwards. It's very important that the butter is at room temperature – not melted – when it is used.

MAKES 16	INGREDIENTS	MAKES 24
½ cup	water	¾ cup
2 tbsp	powdered milk	3 tbsp
½ cup	butter	¾ cup
1 tbsp	sugar	1½ tbsp
1 tsp	salt	1½ tsp
2 cups	bread flour	3 cups
2 tsp	yeast	1 tbsp

GLAZE

1 egg
pinch of salt

METHOD

Put all ingredients except glaze in bread pan in order suggested by your bread machine instructions. Set for white bread, dough stage. Press Start.

Lightly butter two baking sheets.

When dough is ready, remove from bread machine and punch down. Cut the smaller recipe in two pieces, the larger recipe into three pieces. Let dough rest 5 minutes. Roll each piece of dough into a circle about 10 inches in diameter and ⅛ inch thick. To get the dough this thin, you may need to let it relax a little during the rolling.

Cut each circle into eight equal wedges. Take each wedge and roll it one more time with the rolling pin to flatten it. Starting at the wide end of the wedge, roll up the dough toward the point, stretching the dough slightly as you go. Place, with tip under the roll, on baking sheet. Pull ends toward front so the roll forms a crescent.

Make glaze by beating egg and salt together with a fork. Brush croissants with glaze. Cover loosely and set in a warm place to rise until doubled, about 1 hour. Brush again with glaze. Bake in a preheated 375°F oven until golden brown, 20 to 25 minutes.

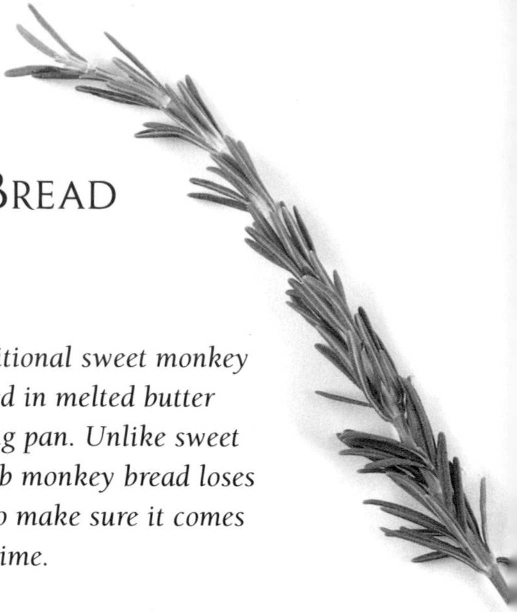

GARLIC HERB MONKEY BREAD

This savory pull-apart bread is a variation on the traditional sweet monkey bread. Small balls of garlic-flavored dough are dipped in melted butter seasoned with garlic and herbs, and layered in a baking pan. Unlike sweet monkey bread, which tastes good hot or cold, garlic-herb monkey bread loses its charm when cold, so time the making of the bread to make sure it comes out of the oven 5 minutes before meal time.

1 lb LOAF	INGREDIENTS	1½ lb LOAF
¾ cup	milk	1½ cups
2 tbsp	vegetable oil	3 tbsp
1 tsp	sugar	1½ tsp
1 tsp	salt	1½ tsp
1	clove garlic, pressed	1 or 2 small
1½ cups	bread flour	2¼ cups
½ cup	whole-wheat flour	¾ cup
1½ tsp	yeast	2¼ tsp
4 tbsp	butter	6 tbsp
2	cloves garlic, pressed	3
¼ tsp	dried sage	¼ tsp
¼ tsp	dried rosemary, crushed	¼ tsp
½ tsp	dried basil	¾ tsp

METHOD

Put first eight ingredients in bread pan in order suggested by your bread machine instructions. Set for whole-wheat bread, dough stage. Press Start.

A few minutes before dough is ready, melt butter in small skillet. Add garlic and herbs. Sauté for 2 minutes. If the garlic or herbs brown too quickly, remove the pan from the heat and let the mixture continue cooking in its own heat. The garlic will give the bread a bitter flavor if it burns. Lightly oil baking dish.

Remove the dough from the bread machine and punch down. Roll dough into a thick log and cut out into 20 to 24 pieces for the small loaf, 30 to 36 pieces for the large loaf. Roll pieces of dough into balls (they do not need to be perfectly round). Dip each ball in butter-herb mixture and layer in baking pan. The pieces in the first layer should be close but not touching to give them room to rise. On each succeeding layer, place balls so they overlap empty spaces on the layer beneath. Drizzle any remaining butter over the dough in the pan.

Cover dough loosely and put it in a warm place to rise. When bread has doubled in volume, about 30 to 40 minutes, put it in preheated 350°F oven. Bake until bread is lightly browned and a skewer inserted comes out clean, about 25 to 30 minutes. Invert bread on serving plate, remove baking pan, and serve.

If you need more time to coincide the baking with serving a meal, you can slow down the rising by putting the assembled bread in the refrigerator, then letting it return to room temperature before baking. Monkey bread is traditionally baked in a tube pan, 10 inches across for the larger loaf, a 7- or 8-inch pan for the smaller loaf. However, it looks impressive and tastes just as good when baked in round casserole dishes, about 1 inch smaller in diameter than the tube pan.

CRISP BREADSTICKS

These thin breadsticks will keep for several days if they are stored in an airtight container.

MAKES 24	INGREDIENTS	MAKES 36
⅔ cup	water	1 cup
¼ cup	vegetable oil	6 tbsp
2 tsp	sugar	1 tbsp
1 tsp	salt	1½ tsp
2 cups	bread flour	3 cups
2 tsp	yeast	1 tbsp
about 2 tbsp	vegetable oil	about 3 tbsp
1	egg white	1
2 tbsp	water	2 tbsp

sesame or poppy seeds or coarse salt, optional

METHOD

Put all but last three ingredients in bread pan in order suggested by your bread machine instructions. Set for white bread, dough stage. Press Start.

Grease 2 or 3 baking sheets.

When dough is ready, remove from bread pan and punch down. Cut smaller batch into 24 pieces, larger batch into 36 pieces. Roll each piece between your palms to form a very skinny rope, about 8 inches long. Place bread sticks 1 inch apart on baking sheets. Brush lightly with oil. Cover loosely and set in a warm place to rise 20 to 25 minutes.

Preheat oven to 350°F. Make wash of egg white and 2 tbsp water. Brush egg wash lightly on bread sticks. Sprinkle with seeds or salt, if desired. Bake until golden brown, about 25 minutes.

SOFT BREADSTICKS

These soft bread sticks do not keep well, but they are delicious still warm from the oven. Sprinkle them with sesame or poppy seeds or coarse salt.

MAKES 20	INGREDIENTS	MAKES 30
10 tbsp	water	1 cup
1	egg, separated	1
2 tbsp	vegetable oil	3 tbsp
2 tsp	sugar	1 tbsp
1 tsp	salt	1½ tsp
2 cups	bread flour	3 cups
1½ tsp	yeast	2¼ tsp
2 tbsp	water	2 tbsp

sesame or poppy seeds or coarse salt, optional

METHOD

Separate the egg and put the yolk in the bread pan. Save the white for glaze. Put remaining ingredients except last 2 tbsp water and seeds in bread pan in order suggested by your bread machine instructions. Set for white bread, dough stage. Press Start.

Grease 2 or 3 baking sheets. Make a wash of the egg white and 2 tbsp water. Preheat oven to 350°F.

When dough is ready, remove from bread machine and punch down. Cut the dough into 20 pieces for the smaller recipe, 30 pieces for the larger recipe. Roll each piece between your palms to form a rope about 6 inches long. Place breadsticks on baking sheet about 1½ inches apart. Brush with egg wash. Sprinkle with seeds or salt, if desired.

Bake breadsticks until golden, 20 to 25 minutes.

HAMBURGER BUNS AND HOT DOG ROLLS

Baking your own hamburger buns or hot dog rolls is as easy as making simple dinner rolls.

MAKES 6	INGREDIENTS	MAKES 9
1	egg	1
½ cup	milk	⅞ cup
3 tbsp	butter	4½ tbsp
2 tbsp	sugar	3 tbsp
½ tsp	salt	¾ tsp
2 cups	bread flour	3 cups
2 tsp	yeast	1 tbsp
2 tbsp	milk	3 tbsp

sesame seeds, optional

METHOD

Put all ingredients except 2 or 3 tbsp milk and sesame seeds in bread pan in order suggested by your bread machine instructions. Set for white bread, dough stage. Press Start.

When dough is ready, remove from bread machine and punch down. Cut smaller recipe into 6 equal pieces, the larger recipe into 9 pieces. Let dough rest 5 minutes while you butter one or two baking sheets. For hamburger buns, roll each piece into a ball and flatten it to form a patty about 3 inches wide and ½ inch thick. For hot dog buns, roll each piece into a 6-inch rope and flatten to ½ inch thickness. Place rolls on baking sheet. Cover loosely and set in a warm place to rise for 20 minutes. Preheat oven to 400°F.

Lightly brush tops of rolls with milk and sprinkle with sesame seeds, if desired. Bake to 12 to 15 minutes, until a skewer inserted in roll comes out clean.

RYE CRESCENT ROLLS

These rye dinner rolls add an elegant touch to any meal, casual or formal. They're so good that they don't need butter.

MAKES 16	INGREDIENTS	MAKES 24
⅔ cup	flat beer	1 cup
2 tbsp	vegetable oil	3 tbsp
1 tbsp	honey	1½ tbsp
1 tsp	salt	1½ tsp
1 tsp	caraway seeds	1½ tsp
1½ cups	bread flour	2¼ cups
¾ cup	rye flour	1⅛ cups
2 tsp	yeast	1 tbsp
2 tbsp	melted butter	3 tbsp

METHOD

Put all ingredients except melted butter in bread pan in order suggested by your bread machine instructions. Set for whole-wheat bread, dough stage. Press Start.

When dough is ready, remove it from the bread machine and punch it down. Cut the smaller recipe into two equal parts, the larger recipe into three parts. Let the dough rest for five minutes. Oil two or three baking sheets.

On a lightly floured surface, roll out the first section of dough into a circle 8 to 9 inches in diameter. Cut the circle into eight wedges. Starting from the outside of the circle and working toward the point, loosely roll up each wedge. Stretch each roll slightly and pull it into a curve. Set it on the baking sheet with the point underneath. Repeat with all the wedges, then with the remaining dough.

Let the dough rise until doubled, about 1 hour. Brush rolls with melted butter. Bake in a preheated 400°F oven until rolls are lightly browned, 12 to 15 minutes.

LEFT Rye Crescent Rolls

SEMOLINA BREAD

Semolina is a hard winter wheat or durum flour used to make pasta, but it also makes a good bread when mixed with other flours. By itself, it makes a very heavy, dense bread. However, this loaf, great with pasta, is light and flavorful.

1 lb LOAF	INGREDIENTS	1½ lb LOAF
¾ cup	water	1⅛ cups
1 tsp	sugar	1½ tsp
1 tsp	salt	1½ tsp
1½ cups	bread flour	2¼ cups
⅔ cup	semolina flour	1 cup
1½ tsp	yeast	2¼ tsp

GLAZE

1 egg yolk beaten with 1 tsp water
2–3 tbsp sesame seeds

METHOD

Put all dough ingredients in bread machine pan. Set for white bread, dough stage. Press Start.

When dough is ready, remove from pan and punch down. Shape it into a fat baguette. Set it on a baking sheet that has been sprinkled with cornmeal. Cover dough and put in a warm place to rise until doubled, about 45 minutes.

Brush loaf with egg glaze and sprinkle with sesame seeds. Bake bread in preheated 375°F oven until golden and bread sounds hollow when rapped on the bottom, about 30 minutes.

Pesto Swirl Bread

A delicious layer of pesto is spread on a light whole-wheat dough, rolled up and baked into a tasty loaf that goes well with soups, salads, pastas, and grilled meat and fish. You can use store-bought pesto or make your own, following the recipe below. It's important that you drain off excess oil from the pesto, but it can be added to the bread instead of plain oil.

1 lb LOAF	INGREDIENTS	1½ lb LOAF
½ cup	water	¾ cup
¼ cup	milk	6 tbsp
1 tbsp	vegetable oil	1½ tbsp
1 tbsp	sugar	1½ tbsp
1 tsp	salt	1½ tsp
1½ cups	bread flour	2¼ cups
½ cup	whole-wheat flour	¾ cup
2 tsp	yeast	1 tbsp
¼ cup	pesto	6 tbsp

METHOD

Put all ingredients except pesto in bread pan in order suggested by your bread machine instructions. Set for whole-wheat bread, dough stage. Press Start.

Butter a 9½-inch loaf pan (large enough for either recipe).

Remove dough from bread machine and punch down. Let it rest 5 minutes. Roll it out on a lightly floured surface to form a rectangle about 8 inches wide and 14 to 18 inches long. Spread pesto evenly over surface. Roll the dough into a fat 8-inch cylinder. Tucking the edge under, put it in the loaf pan. Loosely cover and put in a warm place to rise for 1 hour.

Bake the loaf in a preheated 350°F oven until top is golden and a skewer inserted in the bread comes out clean, 30 to 35 minutes. Remove the bread from the pan and put it on a wire rack to cool for at least 15 minutes.

PESTO

INGREDIENTS

1 cup fresh basil leaves

2 tbsp walnut pieces

1 clove garlic, peeled

¼ cup Parmesan cheese

pinch salt

about 2 tbsp olive oil

METHOD

Put all ingredients except olive oil in blender. Blend, adding a little oil at a time. Keep the pesto rough and fairly dry so that oil doesn't soak into the dough.

WHOLE-WHEAT POTATO CLOVERLEAF ROLLS

*These light whole-wheat rolls are excellent with dinner. If desired, add ½ tsp
dried oregano or dill, or 2 tsp fresh snipped chives.*

MAKES 12-16	INGREDIENTS	MAKES 18-24
½ cup	mashed potatoes	¼ cup
1	egg	1
¼ cup	milk	½ cup
1 tbsp	vegetable oil	1½ tbsp
1 tbsp	sugar	1½ tbsp
1 tsp	salt	1½ tsp
1⅓ cups	bread flour	2 cups
⅔ cup	whole-wheat flour	1 cup
2 tsp	yeast	1 tbsp
about 3 tbsp	melted butter	about 4 tbsp

METHOD

Put all ingredients except melted butter in bread pan in
order suggested by your bread machine instructions. Set
for whole-wheat bread, dough stage. Press Start.

Lightly oil 12 to 16 muffin cups for the smaller recipe,
18 to 24 muffin cups for the larger recipe.

When dough is ready, remove from bread machine and
punch down. Cut smaller recipe into 12 to 16 equal
pieces, the larger recipe into 18 to 24 pieces. Cut each
piece into thirds. Roll each piece into a tiny ball and dip
in the melted butter. Place three tiny balls in each
muffin cup. Cover loosely and set in a warm place to
rise until doubled, 45 minutes to 1 hour.

Preheat oven to 375°F. Lightly brush tops of rolls with
remaining melted butter. Bake 15 to 20 minutes, until
tops are golden brown.

PUMPERNICKEL RAISIN ROLLS

Soft and slightly sweet pumpernickel raisin rolls are delicious with dinner.

MAKES 8-12	INGREDIENTS	MAKES 12-16
1	egg	1
½ cup	milk	⅞ cup
3 tbsp	vegetable oil	4½ tbsp
2 tbsp	molasses	3 tbsp
½ tsp	salt	¾ tsp
2 tbsp	unsweetened cocoa powder	3 tbsp
1 tsp	caraway seeds	1½ tsp
¾ cup	bread flour	1¼ cups
¾ cup	whole-wheat flour	1¼ cups
¾ cup	rye flour	1¼ cups
2 tsp	yeast	1 tbsp
3 tbsp	raisins	4½ tbsp
1 tbsp	melted butter	1½ tbsp

METHOD

Put all ingredients except raisins in bread pan in order suggested by your bread machine instructions. Set for whole-wheat bread, dough stage. Press Start. Add the raisins after the first kneading or when the machine signals it's time to add fruit.

Lightly oil an 8- or 9-inch square pan for the smaller recipe, a 9 × 13-inch pan for the larger recipe.

When dough is ready, remove from bread machine and punch down. Cut smaller recipe into 8 to 12 equal pieces, the larger recipe into 12 to 16 pieces. Roll each piece into a ball – they do not have to be perfectly round. Place balls about ½ inch apart in baking pan. Cover loosely and set in a warm place to rise until doubled, about 1 hour.

Preheat oven to 400°F. Lightly brush tops of rolls with melted butter. Bake 12 to 15 minutes, until a skewer inserted in roll comes out clean.

FRENCH BREAD

This recipe produces wonderful baguettes when still warm, but they become stale within a day.

1 lb LOAF	INGREDIENTS	1½ lb LOAF
¾ cup	water	1 cup
1 tsp	salt	1½ tsp
2 cups	bread flour	3 cups
2 tsp	yeast	1 tbsp

METHOD

Put ingredients in bread pan in order suggested by your bread machine instructions. Set for French bread, medium crust.

To make baguettes, remove dough from bread machine after first kneading and punch down. Cut into two equal pieces. On a lightly floured surface, roll each piece into a thick rope, about 8 inches long for the 1-pound loaf, and 10 inches for the larger loaf. Place on a baking sheet that has been sprinkled with cornmeal. With a sharp knife, cut several diagonal slashes in the top of each loaf. Put dough in a warm place, cover loosely, and let rise until doubled in volume, 45 minutes to 1 hour. Make a wash of 1 tbsp egg white plus 1 tbsp water. Lightly brush wash over surface of loaves. Bake baguettes in preheated 400°F oven for about 25 minutes, until crust is golden brown and bread makes a hollow sound when thumped on the bottom and the top.

For crustier bread, place a shallow pan of boiling water on the bottom shelf of the oven. Or lightly spray water from a spray bottle into the oven when baking begins, and one or two more times during baking.

RIGHT Pumpernickel Raisin Rolls

GARLIC PEPPER POTATO ROLLS

These light dinner rolls are seasoned with garlic and black pepper, and will complement almost any entrée.

MAKES 8-12	INGREDIENTS	MAKES 12-16
1	egg	1 + 1 yolk
3 tbsp	milk	4½ tbsp
½ cup	mashed potatoes	¾ cup
2 tbsp	vegetable oil	3 tbsp
1 tbsp	sugar	1½ tbsp
2	cloves garlic, minced	3
1½ tsp	fresh-ground black pepper	2¼ tsp
1 tsp	salt	1½ tsp
2 cups	bread flour	3 cups
1½ tsp	yeast	2¼ tsp
2 tbsp	milk	3 tbsp

METHOD

Put all ingredients except milk in bread pan in order suggested by your bread machine instructions. Set for white bread, dough stage. Press Start.

Lightly oil an 8- or 9-inch square pan for the smaller recipe, a 9 × 13-inch pan for the larger recipe.

When dough is ready, remove from bread machine and punch down. Cut smaller recipe into 8 to 12 equal pieces, the larger recipe into 12 to 16 pieces. Roll each piece into a ball – it does not have to be perfectly round. Place balls about ½ inch apart in baking pan. Cover loosely and set in a warm place to rise until doubled, 45 minutes to 1 hour.

Preheat oven to 375°F. Lightly brush tops of rolls with milk. Bake 12 to 15 minutes, until rolls are golden and a skewer inserted in roll comes out clean.

ENGLISH MUFFINS

These English muffins are a bit crisper than the soft, store-bought kind, but they have a fresher flavor. The easiest way to make them is with a 3-inch round cookie cutter and a griddle, but you can use a clean tuna or pineapple can and a large skillet.

MAKES 10-12	INGREDIENTS	MAKES 15-18
¼ cup	water	6 tbsp
½ tbsp	baking soda	¼ tsp
½ cup	milk	¼ cup
2 tbsp	vegetable oil	3 tbsp
2 tsp	sugar	1 tbsp
½ tsp	salt	¼ tsp
2 cups	bread flour	3 cups
2 tsp	yeast	1 tbsp
	cornmeal	

METHOD

Dissolve the baking soda in the water. Put the water and remaining ingredients except cornmeal in bread pan in order suggested by your bread machine instructions. Set for white bread, dough stage. Press Start.

Sprinkle cornmeal on a baking sheet or large platter. White cornmeal is more esthetically pleasing on English muffins, but yellow will do the job just fine. When dough is ready, remove it and punch it down and cut it in half. Let it rest 5 minutes. Then on a lightly floured surface, roll out the first half to ⅜ inch thick. With the cookie cutter, cut out 3-inch rounds. Put the rounds on the cornmeal-covered baking sheet, then turn to coat both sides. Repeat with the second half. If you wish, you may roll up the scraps, knead them a little, let the dough rest a few minutes, then roll it out and cut a few more muffins. Don't reroll yet again – the muffins will be tough.

Cover muffins and let them rise 45 minutes.

If you have a griddle, set it for moderate heat. If not, place a skillet – preferably one with a non-stick finish – over moderate heat. If the griddle or pan is well-seasoned, it will not require oil. If not, use just the barest trace of oil to cook. Cook until muffin bottoms are nicely browned, then turn and cook the other side. Cooking time will vary from 6 to 10 minutes per side according to the temperature of your stove.

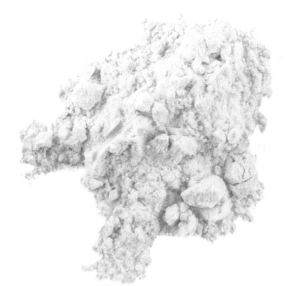

BAGELS

Dense and chewy, bagels are a delight when they are split and toasted and served with butter or cream cheese. They also make delicious sandwiches. You can experiment by adding chopped sautéed onions, or raisins and cinnamon, to the dough.

MAKES 8-10	INGREDIENTS	MAKES 12-15
1	egg	1
½ cup	milk	1 cup
1 tbsp	vegetable oil	1½ tbsp
2 tsp	sugar	1 tbsp
½ tsp	salt	¾ tsp
2 cups	bread flour	3 cups
2 tsp	yeast	1 tbsp
1 tbsp	sugar	1 tbsp
1	egg white	1
2 tsp	water	2 tsp

sesame or poppy seeds or coarse salt

METHOD

Put all but last four ingredients in bread pan in order suggested by your bread machine instructions. Set for white bread, dough stage. Press Start.

When dough is ready, remove from bread machine and punch down. Cut smaller recipe into 8 to 10 equal pieces, the larger recipe into 12 to 15 pieces. Roll each piece between your palms to form a thin rope, about 8 inches long with tapered ends. Bring ends together to form a circle, with the tapered ends overlapping. With moistened fingers, pinch or lightly knead the joined ends so the circle is securely fastened, or it will come apart later.

Set the bagels in a warm place to rise and cover them loosely. They should rise for 15 minutes. Preheat oven to 400°F. While they are rising, bring about 2 quarts of water to boil in a saucepan.
Add 1 tbsp sugar. When the bagels have risen for 15 minutes, drop one or two at a time into the boiling water, handling them as gently as possible so they do not deflate. They will rise to the surface of the water and swell up. Let them cook 1 minute, then turn them over and let them cook 3 minutes longer.

Remove bagels, let drain over the water, and place on an ungreased baking sheet. Beat egg white with water and brush over bagels. Sprinkle with sesame or poppy seeds or coarse salt. Bake until golden, 20 to 25 minutes.

BREADS FROM AROUND THE WORLD

SWEDISH LIMPA BREAD

This is a a slightly sweet rye bread, flavored with a delicious combination of orange peel, anise seed, and caraway seed. It can be used for sandwiches or canapés, but I like it best with only sweet butter.

1 lb LOAF	INGREDIENTS	1½ lb LOAF
¾ cup	water	1¼ cups
1 tbsp	vegetable oil	1½ tbsp
2 tbsp	honey	3 tbsp
1 tsp	salt	1½ tsp
½ tsp	anise seed	¾ tsp
½ tsp	caraway seeds	¾ tsp
1 tbsp	grated orange peel	1½ tbsp
1½ cups	bread flour	2¼ cups
¾ cup	rye flour	1¼ cups
1½ tsp	yeast	2¼ tsp

METHOD

Put ingredients in bread pan in order suggested by your bread machine instructions. Set for whole-wheat bread, medium crust. Press Start.

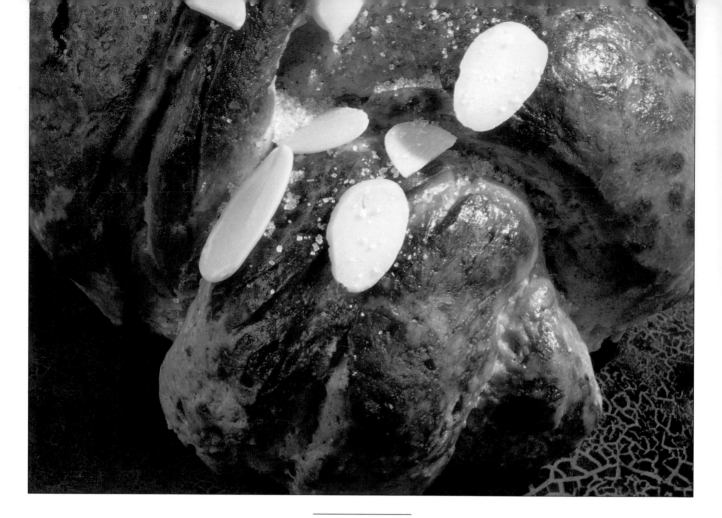

PULLA

Pulla is a Finnish sweet bread seasoned with cardamom, a spice widely used in Scandinavian cooking. It is an everyday bread in Finland, often dressed up with raisins and candied orange peel for holiday celebrations.

1 lb LOAF	INGREDIENTS	1½ lb LOAF
1	egg	1 + 1 yolk
½ cup	milk	¾ cup
2 tbsp	butter	3 tbsp
3 tbsp	sugar	4½ tbsp
½ tsp	salt	¼ tsp
1 tsp	ground cardamom	1½ tsp
2 cups	bread flour	3 cups
2 tsp	yeast	1 tbsp

GLAZE

1 egg white beaten with 2 tsp water
2 tbsp sliced or slivered almonds
1–2 tbsp sugar

METHOD

Put all dough ingredients in bread machine pan. Set for white or sweet bread, dough stage. Press Start.

When dough is ready, take out and punch down. Cut into three equal pieces. Let it rest 5 minutes. Butter a baking sheet. Roll each piece into a rope, about 16 inches for smaller loaf, 20 inches for larger loaf. Braid the ropes, tucking ends under. Cover dough and put in a warm place to rise until doubled.

Brush dough with egg-water wash. Sprinkle with almonds and then with sugar. Bake bread in preheated 375°F oven until golden, about 35 minutes.

VERTERKAKE

This dense, sweet Norwegian bread takes its name from verterol, one of the ingredients in a Norwegian non-alcoholic beer. You can use alcoholic or non-alcoholic beer. This bread, adapted from a James Beard recipe, produces a soft dough that does not cook evenly in the bread machine, so it is baked in a conventional oven.

1 lb LOAF	INGREDIENTS	1½ lb LOAF
½ cup	flat dark beer	¾ cup
⅓ cup	milk	½ cup
2 tbsp	corn syrup	3 tbsp
2 tbsp	sugar	3 tbsp
¼ tsp	ground cloves	½ tsp
¼ tsp	black pepper	½ tsp
½ tsp	salt	¾ tsp
1¼ cups	bread flour	1¾ cups
1 cup	rye flour	1½ cups
1½ tsp	yeast	2¼ tsp
2 tbsp	raisins	3 tbsp

METHOD

Put all ingredients except raisins in bread pan in order suggested by your bread machine instructions. Set for whole-wheat bread, dough stage. Press Start. Add raisins after first kneading or when the machine beeps that it is time to add fruit.

Oil an 8½- to 9½-inch bread pan for the smaller loaf, a 9½- to 10½-inch pan for the larger loaf.

When dough is ready, remove it from the bread machine and punch down. Shape it into a loaf. Place it in the bread pan, then turn so all sides of the dough are oiled. Cover loosely, set it in a warm place, and let it rise until doubled in bulk, 45 minutes to 1 hour.

Brush loaf with hot water and lightly prick the surface with a toothpick. Bake bread in a preheated 375°F oven until loaf browns and sounds hollow when thumped, 35 to 45 minutes.

MOROCCAN BREAD

This is a heavy, coarsely textured bread, fragrant with anise. It is traditionally eaten with tagine, or Moroccan stew.

1 lb LOAF	INGREDIENTS	1½ lb LOAF
¾ cup	water	1¼ cups
¼ tsp	sugar	½ tsp
1½ tsp	anise seed	2¼ tsp
1 tsp	coarse salt	1½ tsp
½ cup	whole-wheat flour	¾ cup
1½ cups	bread flour	2¼ cups
2 tsp	yeast	1 tbsp

METHOD

Put all dough ingredients in bread machine pan. Set for whole-wheat bread, dough stage. Press Start.

When dough is ready, remove from pan and punch down. Shape it into a round loaf and place it on a baking sheet that has been sprinkled with cornmeal. Cover dough and put in a warm place to rise until doubled, 1 to 1½ hours.

Prick dough with a fork. Bake 12 minutes in a preheated 400°F oven, then reduce heat to 300°F and bake about 40 minutes longer, until top and bottom sound hollow when rapped with your knuckles.

BATH BUNS

Bath buns, named after the English city where they originated, are made of a sweet egg dough.

MAKES 8	INGREDIENTS	MAKES 12
1	egg	1 + 1 yolk
½ cup	milk	¾ cup
¼ cup	butter	6 tbsp
¼ cup	sugar	6 tbsp
¼ tsp	ground ginger	½ tsp
¼ tsp	mace	½ tsp
½ tsp	salt	¾ tsp
2 cups	bread flour	3 cups
2 tsp	yeast	1 tbsp
⅓ cup	currants (or raisins)	½ cup

GLAZE

1 egg
1 tbsp milk
1–2 tbsp sugar

METHOD

Put all dough ingredients except currants in bread pan in order suggested by your bread machine instructions. Set for white or sweet bread, dough stage. Press Start. Add the currants after the first kneading or when the machine signals it's time to add fruit.

Butter a baking sheet. When dough is ready, remove from bread machine and punch down. Cut smaller recipe into 8 pieces, the larger recipe into 12. Roll each piece into a ball. Place balls on baking sheet and slightly flatten each one. Cover loosely and set in a warm place to rise until doubled, about 45 minutes.

Preheat oven to 400°F. Make glaze by fork-beating egg and milk. Lightly brush tops of rolls with glaze and sprinkle with sugar. Bake until buns are golden brown, 15 to 20 minutes.

RIGHT Bath Buns

PORTUGUESE SWEET BREAD

This is an eggy, light-textured sweet bread, flavored with vanilla, lemon, and nutmeg. It used to be eaten as an Easter bread in Portugal, but now is eaten as a breakfast bread year-round.

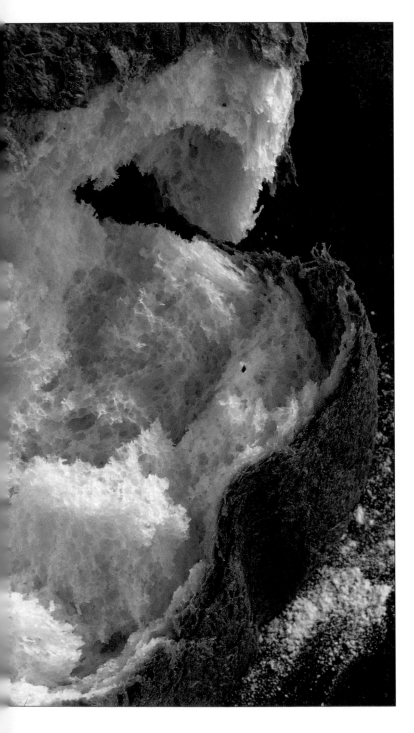

1 lb LOAF	INGREDIENTS	1½ lb LOAF
2	eggs	3
⅓ cup	milk	½ cup
2 tbsp	butter	3 tbsp
3 tbsp	sugar	4½ tbsp
½ tsp	salt	¾ tsp
1 tsp	vanilla	1½ tsp
2 tsp	grated lemon peel	1 tbsp
½ tsp	nutmeg	¾ tsp
2 cups	bread flour	3 cups
1½ tsp	yeast	2¼ tsp

METHOD

Put ingredients in bread pan in order suggested by your bread machine instructions. Set for white or sweet bread, light crust. Press Start.

FOCCACIO

Serve wedges of this hearty bread as an hors d'oeuvre or with a meal instead of garlic bread. Instead of butter, dip pieces in high-quality olive oil. This bread is best served warm.

1 lb LOAF	INGREDIENTS	1½ lb LOAF
⅔ cup	water	1 cup
2 tbsp	olive oil	3 tbsp
1 tsp	salt	1½ tsp
2 cups	bread flour	3 cups
1¼ tsp	yeast	2 tsp
1 or 2	minced garlic cloves	2 or 3
1 tsp	dried rosemary	1½ tsp
1 tsp	coarse salt	1½ tsp
2 tbsp	olive oil	3 tbsp
2 tsp	grated Parmesan	1 tbsp

METHOD

Put first five ingredients in bread pan in order suggested by your bread machine instructions. Set for white bread, dough stage. Press Start.

Preheat oven to 400°F. Lightly sprinkle cornmeal on a baking sheet.

Remove dough and punch down. Let dough rest about 5 minutes. On a lightly floured surface, roll dough into a round, about ½ inch thick. Place dough on baking sheet. Sprinkle the garlic, rosemary, and coarse salt over the top, then lightly press it into the dough. With your fingertips, poke shallow indentations all over the top of the round. Pour the remaining olive oil over the top, letting it pool in the indentations. Sprinkle Parmesan over the top.

Bake bread until lightly browned, about 20 minutes.

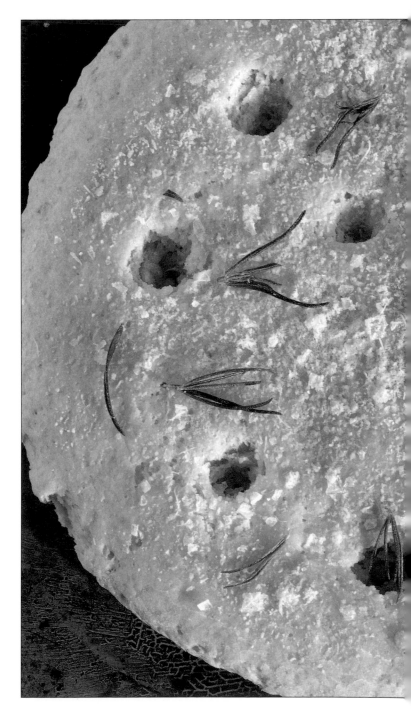

BOLILLOS

These Mexican rolls are large and crusty, excellent with dinner.

MAKES 6	INGREDIENTS	MAKES 9
⅔ cup	water	1 cup
1 tsp	sugar	1½ tsp
1 tsp	salt	1½ tsp
2 cups	bread flour	3 cups
1½ tsp	yeast	2¼ tsp

GLAZE

1 egg
1 tbsp water

METHOD

Put all ingredients except glaze in bread pan in order suggested by your bread machine instructions. Set for white bread, dough stage. Press Start.

Lightly oil a baking sheet.

When dough is ready, remove from bread machine and punch down. Cut smaller recipe into 6 equal pieces, the larger recipe into 9 pieces. Roll each piece into a ball. Flatten ball, then gently stretch and elongate to form an oval. Now, working on the long sides of the oval, fold those sides in toward the middle. Roll and stretch so the center is thick and the ends are tapered like a spindle. Place the rolls, seam side down, on the baking sheet. Cover loosely and set in a warm place to rise until doubled, about 1 hour.

Preheat oven to 400°F. Lightly brush rolls with egg glaze. With a sharp knife or razor blade, make two diagonal slashes in the top of each roll. Bake 15 to 20 minutes, until rolls are golden and crusty.

PITA BREAD

These rounds of dough puff up when they are baked at high temperature. Cut open an edge to create pockets that can be stuffed with all kinds of fillings.

MAKES 6	INGREDIENTS	MAKES 9
¾ cup	water	1¼ cups
1 tbsp	olive oil	1½ tbsp
1 tsp	sugar	1½ tsp
1 tsp	salt	1½ tsp
1⅓ cups	bread flour	2 cups
⅔ cup	whole-wheat flour	1 cup
1½ tsp	yeast	2¼ tsp

METHOD

Put ingredients in bread pan in order suggested by your bread machine instructions and set for whole-wheat, dough stage.

Punch down dough and cut into 6 equal pieces for smaller recipe, 9 pieces for the larger one. Roll each piece between your hands to form a ball. Flatten slightly and let dough rest about 10 minutes. This will let the dough relax so it will stretch more readily when you roll it out, rather than bouncing back. On a lightly floured surface, roll out each circle of dough to a diameter of about 6 inches. Use flour sparingly, as too much flour will interfere with the moisture that creates steam and causes the dough to puff up. Cover the dough with plastic wrap or a barely damp towel, and let the dough rise about 30 minutes, until it is puffy.

Preheat oven to 475°F. Lightly sprinkle cornmeal on a baking sheet. When dough is ready, carefully transfer rounds to the baking sheet. Bake until dough puffs up and is lightly browned, 5 to 6 minutes, then turn and bake until other side is lightly browned, about 2 minutes.

BRIOCHE

This buttery bread is not quite the same as the classic French brioche baked in a fluted pan, but is a deliciously close cousin. Although it makes good sandwiches, it is best served simply, toasted or untoasted, with butter.

1 lb LOAF	INGREDIENTS	1½ lb LOAF
¼ cup	water	6 tbsp
2	eggs	3
⅓ cup	butter	½ cup
1 tbsp	sugar	1½ tbsp
½ tsp	salt	¾ tsp
2 cups	bread flour	3 cups
1½ tsp	yeast	2¼ tsp

METHOD

Put ingredients in bread pan in order suggested by your bread machine instructions. It is crucial that the butter is softened to room temperature – not melted – when it is added to the other ingredients. Set for white bread, medium crust. Press Start.

Pistolet

Pistolets are split rolls made in France and Belgium. Traditionally the dough is allowed to rise for several hours on the first rising to develop the flavor, then rise twice more. The dough is shaped into a plum-sized ball, then nearly split with the handle of a wooden spoon.

MAKES 15	INGREDIENTS	MAKES 22
¾ cup	water	1¼ cups
3 tbsp	powdered milk	4½ tbsp
2 tbsp	butter	3 tbsp
1 tbsp	sugar	1½ tbsp
1 tsp	salt	1½ tsp
2 cups	bread flour	3 cups
1½ tsp	yeast	2¼ tsp
¼ cup	rye flour	⅓ cup

METHOD

Put all ingredients except rye flour in bread pan in order suggested by your bread machine instructions. Set for white bread, dough stage. Press Start.

If your machine does not punch down the dough for you at this point, or if you can stop the machine, remove the pan. Cover it loosely, put it in a warm place and let dough continue rising for another two hours. It will have tripled in volume, and yeast flavors will have developed.

Punch the dough down and let it rise again for 45 minutes. Butter a baking sheet.

When dough is ready, punch it down. Cut smaller recipe into about 15 equal pieces, the larger recipe into about 22 pieces. Roll each piece into a ball. Dust the top with rye flour. Oil the dowel-like wooden handle of a large spoon. Use the handle to split each ball almost in half. The two sides of the ball should still be connected by a narrow strip of dough. Hold each pistolet at each end of the split with your thumbs in the trough. Pull gently to elongate the roll, and the sides will almost come together.

Traditionally, the roll is placed top (seam-side) down on the baking sheet. After it has risen, it is turned upright and baked. However, if you are all thumbs and tend to deflate the dough when you handle it, just leave it upright and let it rise with the seam side up. Cover them up loosely, put in a warm place, and let them rise for 30 minutes.

Preheat oven to 425°F. Pour boiling water into a shallow baking pan and place it on the bottom shelf of the oven. The steam will give the pistolets a crusty finish. Bake pistolets until they are golden brown and crusty, 15 to 20 minutes.

LAVOSH (ARMENIAN FLATBREAD)

Lavosh is a puffy flatbread that is crisper than pita bread, but softer than a cracker. Rounds of lavosh are broken into pieces, not cut. Eat lavosh plain or with butter.

MAKES 4	INGREDIENTS	MAKES 6
¼ cup	water	1¼ cups
3 tbsp	butter	4½ tbsp
1 tsp	salt	1½ tsp
2 cups	bread flour	3 cups
1½ tsp	yeast	2¼ tsp
1	egg	1
2 tbsp	water	3 tbsp
1–2 tsp	sesame or poppy seeds	2–3 tsp

METHOD

Put water, butter, salt, flour, and yeast in bread pan in order suggested by your bread machine instructions. Set for white bread, dough stage.

Remove dough and punch down. Cut into 4 pieces for smaller recipe, 6 pieces for larger recipe. Roll each piece between your hands to form a ball, then flatten each ball slightly. Let dough relax for 10 minutes or so. This will help the dough stretch when you roll it out. Otherwise, it will keep bouncing back to its original shape.

Preheat oven to 400°F. Make a wash by lightly beating egg with remaining water.

On a lightly floured surface, roll out the first round of dough until it is paper thin. Transfer to a greased baking sheet. Working quickly, brush it with the egg wash. Sprinkle with seeds. Put the first round in the oven immediately, and repeat the process with each round. Bake each lavosh until it is puffy and lightly browned, 8 to 12 minutes.

Sourdough Breads

SOURDOUGH STARTER

*Sourdough is the product of fermentation in dough that has been allowed to
sit out for days and gather wild yeasts from the air. In ancient times, it was
the only leavening known to bread bakers, and much effort was made to
disguise its sour taste. It came back into common usage in mining camps
during the California Gold Rush of 1849, then hit a new wave of popularity
in the middle of the 20th century. Now the tang of sourdough is a favorite
addition to many breads, from waffles to English muffins to rye bread, and
the most popular, a dense sourdough French bread.
Making and maintaining your own sourdough starter is not difficult.
A pot of starter takes at least a few days to ferment and develop a sour
flavor before you add it to the first loaf, but after that, it can be
used and replenished daily.*

INGREDIENTS

1 cup low-fat milk, scalded
1 cup hot water
1 tbsp sugar
2¼ tsp active dry yeast
2½ cups all-purpose flour or bread flour

METHOD

Mix the milk, water, and sugar. When the temperature
has cooled to between 105°F and 115°F, add the yeast.
Allow the yeast to develop a foamy head, a process that
takes 5 to 10 minutes. Then add it to the flour and mix
well.

Put the bowl in a warm place, between 80°F and 100°F,
like the back of the stove. Loosely cover the bowl so
that air will still circulate and the starter will gather
airborne yeasts. Within 24 hours, it should be bubbly
and have the beginnings of a sour smell. Stir it once or
twice a day. The starter may separate into a thick, curd-
like mixture on the bottom and gray watery liquids on
the top. That's normal, as long as it doesn't
turn green or pink. (If it does, throw it out and start

again.) The mixture is ready to use when it develops a
good sour smell, usually three to five days.

To bake sourdough bread, you need to prepare a sponge
at least six hours in advance. Mix some starter with a
portion of flour and liquid, as directed by the recipe.
Replenish the starter with amounts of flour and water
equal to the amount you removed. For instance, if the
recipe calls for ½ cup of sourdough starter, replenish the
starter with ½ cup water and ½ cup flour. Both the
sponge and the replenished starter should be put in a
warm place, covered loosely, and left to ferment at least
6 hours, until bubbly.

If you use the sourdough on an almost daily basis, you
can leave the starter pot at the back of the stove,
replenishing it after each use. It you are only an
occasional baker, replenish it, let it sit out for 6 to 24
hours, then put the starter in the refrigerator. The starter
pot should be tightly covered when it is in the
refrigerator. If you do not bake at least once a week,
refresh the starter every week or two. Remove 1 cup of
starter and discard the rest. Add 1 cup of water and 1 cup
of flour and return it to the refrigerator.

SOURDOUGH WALNUT RYE BREAD

This bread is good for meat or cheese sandwiches. Use walnut oil if you have it, otherwise substitute vegetable oil. Because the bread uses sourdough starter, the sponge should be made the night before baking.

1 lb LOAF	INGREDIENTS	1½ lb LOAF
½ cup	sourdough starter	¼ cup
7 tbsp	water	⅔ cup
1 tbsp	walnut or vegetable oil	1½ tbsp
1 tbsp	sugar	1½ tbsp
1 tsp	salt	1½ tsp
2 tbsp	cornmeal	3 tbsp
1 cup	rye flour	1½ cups
1 cup	bread flour	1½ cups
2 tsp	yeast	1 tbsp
⅓ cup	chopped walnuts	½ cup

METHOD

To make sponge, combine sourdough starter, ¼ cup of the water and ½ cup of the rye flour. Stir well. Cover it loosely and set it in a warm place to ferment overnight.

Put the sponge and all remaining ingredients except walnuts in bread pan in order suggested by your bread machine instructions. Set for whole-wheat bread, medium crust. Press Start. Add walnuts after the first kneading or at the beeper.

SOURDOUGH RYE BREAD

This rye bread makes great sandwiches. It can be baked in the bread machine, but is also good baked in the oven.

1 lb LOAF	INGREDIENTS	1½ lb LOAF
¼ cup	sourdough starter	6 tbsp
⅔ cup	water	1 cup
¾ cup	rye flour	1¼ cups
2 tsp	caraway seeds	1 tbsp
1 tbsp	vegetable oil	1½ tsp
1 tbsp	sugar	1½ tbsp
1 tsp	salt	1½ tsp
1⅔ cups	bread flour	2 cups
2 tsp	yeast	1 tbsp

METHOD

The night before baking bread, make a sponge by combining the sourdough starter, ⅓ cup water (½ cup for larger loaf), rye flour, and 1 tsp caraway seeds. Cover loosely and set in a warm place for at least 8 hours.

Put sponge and remaining ingredients in a bread pan in order suggested by your bread machine instructions. Set for whole-wheat bread, medium crust. Press Start.

To bake bread in a conventional oven, set the machine for the dough stage. Remove when dough is ready, punch down. Shape into a long, fat loaf or a round loaf. Place on a baking sheet slightly sprinkled with cornmeal. Cover loosely and put in a warm place to rise until doubled in volume, about 1 hour.

When bread has risen, make a wash of 1 lightly beaten egg and 1 tbsp water. Lightly brush the wash over the surface of the loaf, taking care not to deflate the dough. Bake bread in a preheated 350°F oven until bread is crusty and makes a hollow sound when tapped on the top and bottom.

SOURDOUGH WHOLE-WHEAT BREAD

This is a dense and flavorful bread, but it is not a high-riser.

1lb LOAF	INGREDIENTS	1½ lb LOAF
⅓ cup	sourdough starter	½ cup
⅓ cup	water	½ cup
¼ cup	cracked wheat	6 tbsp
2 tbsp	butter	3 tbsp
1 tbsp	honey	1½ tbsp
2 tbsp	dried milk	3 tbsp
1 tsp	salt	1½ tsp
1 cup	bread flour	1½ cups
1 cup	whole-wheat flour	1½ cups
1½ tsp	yeast	2¼ tsp

METHOD

The night before making bread, make the sponge by mixing sourdough starter, ½ cup bread flour, and about 2 tbsp water. Cover loosely and put in a warm place for at least 6 hours.

About 20 minutes before starting bread, put the cracked wheat in a small saucepan. Cover with water. Bring to a boil, then boil 6 minutes. Drain the wheat thoroughly, then let it cool at least 10 minutes.

Stir down the sponge and put it in the bread machine pan with the remainder of the water. Add cooled wheat and remaining ingredients in the order suggested by your bread machine instructions. Set for whole-wheat bread, medium crust. Press Start.

RIGHT Sourdough Whole-Wheat Bread

SOURDOUGH FRENCH BREAD

Sourdough bread can be both stubborn and temperamental, but it is also delicious. Unlike most of the other sourdough recipes in this book, the sourdough starter in this bread is a major ingredient, not just a small addition for extra flavor. The flavor will vary according to the type of sourdough starter you use and the airborne wild yeasts in your area. Because the sponge sits out for at least eight hours and absorbs moisture from the air, the amount of water you add may also vary.

1 lb LOAF	INGREDIENTS	1½ lb LOAF
⅔ cup	sourdough starter	1 cup
¼ cup	water	6 tbsp
2 tsp	sugar	1 tbsp
1 tsp	salt	1½ tsp
1¼ cups	bread flour	2⅓ cups
2 tsp	yeast	1 tbsp
1 tsp	cornstarch	1½ tsp
2 tbsp	water	3 tbsp

METHOD

The day before you bake the bread, make the sponge by mixing the starter, ¾ cup flour, and 2 tbsp water. Cover loosely and put in a warm place. Let sit at least 8 hours.

Put sponge, 2 tbsp water, sugar, salt, remaining flour, and yeast in bread pan in order suggested by your bread machine instructions. Set for French or white bread, dough stage. Press Start.

When dough is ready, remove from bread machine and punch down. Shape the dough into one short, fat loaf, one round loaf, or one baguette for the smaller recipe, two baguettes for the large one. Place loaf on baking sheet that has been sprinkled with cornmeal. Use a sharp knife to cut several diagonal slashes in the top. Cover bread loosely and set it in a warm place to rise. This is a slow-rising bread which may take an hour or longer.

Preheat oven to 400°F. When bread has risen, dissolve cornstarch in 2 tbsp water and lightly brush it over the surface of the bread. For crustier bread, place a shallow pan of boiling water on the bottom shelf of the oven, or use a spray bottle to squirt water into the oven several times while baking. Bake 35 to 40 minutes, until crust is browned and bread makes hollow sound on top and bottom when rapped with knuckles.

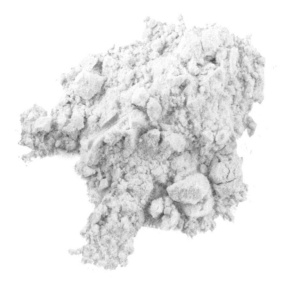

COFFEE CAKES, SWEET BREADS, AND DOUGHNUTS

CINNAMON STICKY BUNS

These sweet, sticky buns can be assembled in advance and refrigerated overnight. In the morning, they will have to finish their second rising before you bake them.

MAKES 15	INGREDIENTS	MAKES 22
	DOUGH	
½ cup	milk	⅞ cup
1	egg	1
3 tbsp	butter	4½ tbsp
¼ cup	sugar	6 tbsp
½ tsp	salt	¾ tsp
2 cups	bread flour	3 cups
2 tsp	yeast	1 tbsp
	FILLING	
⅓ cup	brown sugar	½ cup
1 tsp	cinnamon	1½ tsp
2 tbsp	very soft butter	3 tbsp
	SYRUP	
3 tbsp	butter	4½ tbsp
½ cup	brown sugar	¾ cup
2 tbsp	water	3 tbsp
30	pecan halves	44

METHOD

Put dough ingredients in bread pan in order suggested by your bread machine instructions. Set for white or sweet bread, dough stage. Press Start.

Remove the dough from the bread machine and punch down. Let it rest for 5 minutes to make it easier to roll out. While dough is relaxing, mix brown sugar and cinnamon to make filling. For the smaller recipe, roll dough into a rectangle 7 to 8 inches wide and about 16 inches long. For the larger recipe, cut down in half and roll into two rectangles, each 7 to 8 inches wide and 11

to 12 inches long. Spread the soft butter over the surface of the dough. Thickly sprinkle brown sugar and cinnamon over the surface, spreading to edges. Roll dough into a long cylinder or cylinders. Slicing crosswise through the cylinder, cut into 15 pieces for the smaller recipe, 22 pieces for the larger.

The rolls can be baked together in baking pans or separately in muffin pans. The muffin-pan rolls are neater and crusty on the outside. If you cook them in baking pans, they will be softer. An 8-inch square baking pan is the perfect size for nine rolls; a 9 × 13-inch pan should hold 15 rolls.

Make the syrup by combining butter, brown sugar, and water in a small pan. Heat until butter is melted and sugar is dissolved. Stir well, then pour syrup into the bottoms of the baking pan or muffin-pan cups. Place two pecan halves in the bottom of each muffin cup, or on the top of each roll if you are using a baking pan. Place rolls in muffin cups, or turn them upside down (so pecans are on the bottom) in a baking pan. Cover rolls loosely, set them in a warm place, and let them rise until doubled, 45 minutes to 1 hour.

Bake rolls in a preheated 350°F oven until they are nicely browned, 17 to 22 minutes in a muffin pan, 20 to 25 minutes in a baking pan. The rolls must be removed from the pan immediately, or the sugar syrup will harden. Keeping in mind that excess sugar syrup will run off, invert the pan or muffin pan over a large plate or baking sheet. Let them cool slightly, or the hot sugar will burn your mouth.

KUGELHOPF

This is an Austrian bread reputedly brought to France by Marie Antoinette. It is a sweet, fruit-studded batter bread and will not cook evenly in the bread machine, so must be baked in the oven. It is considered so special a bread that a fluted tube pan was created for it, but a bundt pan or angel-food cake pan will do nicely.

1 lb LOAF	INGREDIENTS	1½ lb LOAF
2 + 1 yolk	eggs	4 eggs
3 tbsp	milk	⅓ cup
⅓ cup	butter	½ cup
3½ tbsp	sugar	⅓ cup
½ tsp	vanilla	1 tsp
2 tsp	grated lemon peel	1 tbsp
½ tsp	salt	1 tsp
2 cups	bread flour	3 cups
2 tsp	yeast	1 tbsp
¼ cup	raisins	¾ cup
⅓ cup	slivered almonds	½ cup
	confectioner's sugar	

METHOD

Put all ingredients except raisins, almonds, and confectioner's sugar in bread pan in order suggested by your bread machine instructions. Set for white or sweet bread, dough stage. Press Start. Add raisins and almonds at the beeper or after the first kneading.

Remove the dough from the bread machine and punch down. Let it rest for 5 minutes. Butter a 6-cup tube pan for the smaller loaf, a 9-cup tube pan for the larger loaf. Put the dough in the pan and spread it around evenly. Cover loosely and put in a warm place to rise 45 minutes to 1 hour.

Bake kugelhopf in a preheated 350°F oven until a skewer inserted in bread comes out clean, 35 to 40 minutes. Let cool 10 minutes, then invert on cooling rack. Dust with confectioner's sugar while kugelhopf is still warm.

ORANGE MONKEY BREAD

This sweet pull-apart bread is a favorite breakfast treat. Small balls of sweet, orange-flavored dough are dipped in a melted butter seasoned with orange liqueur, dipped in cinnamon and sugar, and layered in a baking pan. The bread is wonderful when warm, but still tastes good at room temperature. Time the making of the bread so it comes out of the oven 10 to 15 minutes before meal time.

1 lb LOAF	INGREDIENTS	1½ lb LOAF
⅔ cup	milk	1 cup
2 tbsp	butter	3 tbsp
2 tbsp	sugar	3 tbsp
½ tsp	salt	¾ tsp
2 tsp	grated orange peel	1 tbsp
2 cups	bread flour	3 cups
1½ tsp	yeast	2¼ tsp
3 tbsp	melted butter	4½ tbsp
2 tbsp	orange liqueur or orange juice	3 tbsp
1 cup	sugar	1½ cups
1 tsp	cinnamon	1½ tsp

METHOD

Put first seven ingredients in bread pan in order suggested by your bread machine instructions. Set for white or sweet bread, dough stage. Press Start.

Lightly butter baking dish. A few minutes before dough is ready, melt butter. Stir in orange juice or orange liqueur. In a separate bowl, mix the cinnamon and sugar. Put about half of the cinnamon and sugar in another bowl. Each time you dip a buttery ball into the sugar, it will drip a little of the butter into the sugar, and the sugar will become hard to work with. Then replenish it with some of the reserved cinnamon and sugar.

Remove the dough from the bread machine and punch down. Roll dough into a thick log and cut it into 20 to 24 pieces for the small loaf, 30 to 36 pieces for the large loaf. Roll pieces of dough into balls (they do not need to be perfectly round). Dip each ball in butter-orange

mixture, then in cinnamon-sugar and layer in baking pan. Note: the pieces in the first layer should be close but not touching to give them room to rise. On each succeeding layer, place balls so they overlap empty spaces on the layer beneath. You can put the assembled bread in the refrigerator the night before, and it will rise a little overnight. Let the dough return to room temperature and finish rising, then bake. Monkey bread is traditionally baked in a tube pan, 10 inches across for the larger loaf, a 7- or 8-inch pan for the smaller loaf. However, it looks impressive and tastes just as good when baked in round casserole dishes, about 1 inch smaller in diameter than the tube pans.

Drizzle any remaining butter and cinnamon-sugar over the dough in the pan. Cover it loosely, and put it in a warm place to rise. When bread has doubled in volume, about 30 to 40 minutes, put it in preheated 350°F oven. Bake until bread is lightly browned and a skewer inserted in the bread comes out clean, about 25 to 30 minutes. Invert bread on serving plate, being very careful of the hot syrup that has collected at the bottom of the pan. (Drain off excess syrup first, if desired, or let the syrup run onto the plate.) Remove baking pan, let it cool a little, and serve.

CINNAMON RAISIN SWIRL BREAD

This is an easy breakfast bread that tastes like cinnamon rolls, although it is not as gooey. It is delicious warm and doesn't need butter. The bread can be assembled the night before, then left to rise in the refrigerator overnight.

1 lb LOAF	INGREDIENTS	1½ lb LOAF
¾ cup	milk	1¼ cups
1 tbsp	butter	1½ tbsp
3 tbsp	sugar	4½ tbsp
1 tsp	salt	1½ tsp
2 cups	bread flour	3 cups
2 tsp	yeast	1 tbsp
¼ cup	raisins	6 tbsp
1½ tbsp	very soft butter	2 tbsp
¼ cup	brown sugar	6 tbsp
1 tsp	cinnamon	1½ tsp

METHOD

Put first six ingredients in bread pan in order suggested by your bread machine instructions. Set for white or sweet bread, dough stage. Press Start. Add the raisins after the first kneading or when the beep sounds to add fruit.

Remove butter from refrigerator to soften it. Mix brown sugar and cinnamon. Butter a 9½-inch loaf pan (large enough for either recipe).

Remove dough from bread machine and punch down. Let it rest 5 minutes. Roll it out on a lightly floured surface to form a rectangle about 8 inches wide and about 16 inches long. Spread the butter, then sprinkle the brown sugar mixture over the surface of the dough. Roll it into a fat 8-inch-long cylinder. Tucking the edge under, put it in the loaf pan. Loosely cover and put in a warm place to rise for 1 hour.

Bake the loaf in a preheated 350°F oven until top is golden and a skewer inserted in the bread comes out clean, 25 to 30 minutes. Remove the bread from the pan and put it on a wire rack. Let it cool at least 30 minutes so the hot sugar does not burn you.

BEIGNETS

These small, diamond-shaped doughnuts are a staple in New Orleans, where they are traditionally eaten warm with café au lait.

MAKES 4 DOZEN	INGREDIENTS	MAKES 6 DOZEN
⅔ cup	milk	1¼ cups
1	egg	1
½ tsp	vanilla	¾ tsp
2 tbsp	butter	3 tbsp
¼ cup	sugar	6 tbsp
½ tsp	salt	¾ tsp
¼ tsp	nutmeg	½ tsp
2½ cups	bread flour	3¾ cups
1½ tsp	yeast	2¼ tsp

oil for frying
confectioner's sugar

METHOD

Put all ingredients except oil and confectioner's sugar in bread pan in order suggested by your bread machine instructions. Set for white bread, dough stage. Press Start.

When dough is ready, punch down. Let it rest about 5 minutes. Then, on a lightly floured surface, roll dough into a rectangle about ½ inch thick. Working at a diagonal to the edge of the rectangle, cut dough into 1½-inch strips. Then cut the strips into diamonds with a new series of cuts, almost but not quite perpendicular to the first. Place the diamonds on ungreased baking sheets. Cover loosely and put them in a warm place to rise for 45 minutes.

Pour oil at least 3 inches deep into a deep skillet, wok, or saucepan. Heat oil to 365°F. Watch the oil temperature carefully, as it can climb quickly. Slide a few beignets into the hot oil. Do not crowd them. They will bob back up to the surface. Cook until golden on the bottom, 2 to 3 minutes. Then turn and cook another 2 to 3 minutes on the other side. You may need to hold the beignets down with a large spoon or other cooking utensil to keep them from turning uncooked side up again.

When beignets are golden, remove them from the oil, letting them drain for a few moments over the oil. Then put them on several layers of paper towels. Sprinkle them with confectioner's sugar. Beignets should be served warm. You may put the cooked beignets in a warm oven while others are cooking. Make sure the oil temperature returns to 365°F before you add the next batch of beignets.

CALAS

Calas are rice fritters made with a yeast dough and fried like small doughnuts. The grains of cooked rice disappear into the delicious puffs of fried dough.

MAKES 30	INGREDIENTS	MAKES 45
2	eggs	3
2 tsp	vanilla	1 tbsp
6 tbsp	sugar	½ cup
½ tsp	salt	¼ tsp
½ tsp	nutmeg	¼ tsp
½ tsp	grated lemon peel	¼ tsp
2 cups	cooked, cooled rice	3 cups
2 cups	bread flour	3 cups
1 tsp	yeast	1½ tsp
	oil for frying	
	confectioner's sugar	

METHOD

Put all ingredients except oil and confectioner's sugar in bread pan in order suggested by your bread machine instructions. Set for white bread, dough stage. Press Start.

When dough is ready, punch down. Let it rest about 5 minutes. Then cut off walnut-sized pieces and place them on a greased baking sheet. (Lightly flour your hands, if necessary, to work with the sticky batter.) Cover loosely and put them in a warm place to rise for 1 hour.

Pour oil at least 3 inches deep into a deep skillet, wok, or saucepan. Heat oil to 365°F. Watch the oil temperature carefully, as it can climb quickly. Slide a few rice balls into the hot oil. Do not crowd them. They will bob back up to the surface. Cook until golden on the bottom, about 2 minutes. Then turn and cook another 2 minutes on the other side.

When fritters are golden, remove them from the oil, letting them drain for a few moments over the oil. Then put them on several layers of paper towels. Sprinkle them with confectioner's sugar. Calas should be served warm. You may put the cooked calas in a warm oven while others are cooking. Make sure the oil temperature returns to 365°F before you add the next batch of calas.

RAISED DOUGHNUTS

*Coated in sugar or drizzled with a sugar glaze, these doughnuts
are delicious.*

MAKES 8-10	INGREDIENTS	MAKES 12-15
½ cup	milk	⅞ cup
1	egg	1
2 tbsp	butter	3 tbsp
¼ cup	sugar	6 tbsp
½ tsp	salt	¾ tsp
2 cups	bread flour	3 cups
1½ tsp	yeast	2¼ tsp
	oil for frying	

CHOICE OF SUGAR COATINGS

confectioner's sugar
granulated cinnamon and sugar
sugar glaze (see below)

SUGAR GLAZE

¾ cup confectioner's sugar
½ tsp vanilla
1 tbsp warm milk

METHOD

Put all ingredients except oil and sugar coating in bread pan in order suggested by your bread machine instructions. Set for white bread, dough stage. Press Start.

When dough is ready, punch down. Let it rest about 5 minutes. Then, on a lightly floured surface, roll dough into a rectangle about ⅜ inch thick. Using a doughnut cutter or a 3-inch cookie cutter, cut out doughnuts. If you are not using a doughnut cutter, cut out a ½-inch hole in the center. Knead scraps together and let rest 5 minutes. Reroll the dough and cut out more doughnuts. Place the doughnuts on ungreased baking sheets. Cover loosely and put them in a warm place to rise 45 minutes to 1 hour, until doubled in bulk.

About 15 minutes before doughnuts finish rising, pour oil at least 3 inches deep into a deep skillet, wok, or saucepan. Heat oil to 365°F. Watch the oil temperature carefully, as it can climb quickly. Slide two or three doughnuts into the hot oil. Do not crowd them. Cook until golden on the bottom, 1½ to 2½ minutes. Then turn and cook the other side.

When doughnuts are golden, remove them from the oil, letting them drain for a few moments over the oil. Then put them on several layers of paper towels. Make sure the oil temperature returns to 365°F before you add the next batch of doughnuts.

Put confectioner's sugar or a mixture of cinnamon and granulated sugar in a paper bag with two doughnuts. Shake until they are coated. Remove and repeat until all doughnuts are coated.

Alternatively, mix the ingredients for the sugar glaze together and drizzle it over the tops of the doughnuts.

KOLACHE

Kolaches are individual Czechoslovakian pastries with fruit or cheese fillings, often eaten at Easter or Christmas. Below are recipes for two fillings, or you can use your favorite recipe for other fruit, nut, or poppyseed fillings. For special occasions, serve a variety of fillings.

MAKES 16	INGREDIENTS	MAKES 24
1	egg	1 + 1 yolk
½ cup	milk	¾ cup
50 g (2 oz)	butter	85 g (3 oz)
¼ cup	sugar	6 tbsp
½ tsp	salt	¾ tsp
2 cups	bread flour	3 cups
1½ tsp	yeast	2¼ tsp
	confectioner's sugar	

APRICOT FILLING
(Makes enough for 16 kolaches)

½ cup chopped dried apricots

⅓ cup sugar

2 tbsp apricot brandy, orange liqueur or orange juice

CHEESE FILLING
(Makes enough for 24 kolaches)

3 oz cream cheese, softened

⅔ cup ricotta cheese, watery liquids poured off

1 egg yolk

3 tbsp sugar

½ tsp fresh lemon juice

METHOD

Put all ingredients in bread pan in order suggested by your bread machine instructions. Set for white bread, dough stage. Press Start.

Lightly oil two baking sheets.

When dough is ready, remove from bread machine and punch down. Cut smaller recipe into 16 equal pieces, the larger recipe into 24 pieces. Roll each piece into a ball and flatten slightly. Place balls about 1 inch apart in baking pan. Cover loosely and set in a warm place to rise until doubled, about 45 minutes.

Preheat oven to 375°F. Gently use one finger to make an indentation in the top of each kolache, taking care not to deflate the roll. Gently widen the hole with your finger. Put about 1 tbsp of filling (see below) in each kolache. Bake until kolaches are golden brown, 15 to 20 minutes. Sprinkle with confectioner's sugar while still warm.

APRICOT FILLING

Put apricots in a small saucepan. Cover with water. Bring to a boil, then reduce heat to very low. Simmer until water evaporates, watching closely and stirring frequently so apricots do not scorch. Just as last bit of water evaporates, add sugar and liqueur and heat just until sugar dissolves, about 1 minute. Let cool slightly, then purée in blender or food processor.

CHEESE FILLING

Beat all ingredients together until smooth.

SOPAIPILLAS

These Mexican treats are coated with sugar and served with honey.

MAKES 16	INGREDIENTS	MAKES 25
⅓ cup	water	½ cup
⅓ cup	milk	½ cup
1 tbsp	lard or solid shortening	1½ tbsp
1 tbsp	sugar	1½ tbsp
½ tsp	salt	¾ tsp
2 cups	bread flour	3 cups
1½ tsp	yeast	2¼ tsp
	oil for frying	
	confectioner's sugar	

METHOD

Put all ingredients except oil and confectioner's sugar in bread pan in order suggested by your machine's instructions. Set for white bread, dough stage. Press Start.

When dough is ready, punch down. Let it rest about 5 minutes. Then, on a lightly floured surface, roll dough into a rectangle about ⅜ inch thick. Cut dough into 2-inch squares. Place squares on ungreased baking sheets. Cover loosely and put in a warm place to rise while you heat the oil, about 15 minutes.

Pour oil at least 3 inches deep into a deep skillet, wok, or saucepan. Heat oil to 350°F. Watch the oil temperature carefully, as it can climb quickly. Slide a few sopaipillas into the hot oil. Do not crowd them. Cook until golden, turning once. Total cooking time is 1½ to 2 minutes.

Remove sopaipillas from the oil, letting them drain for a few moments. Then put them on several layers of paper towels. Sprinkle with confectioner's sugar, or put sugar and sopaipillas in a paper bag and shake. Make sure the oil temperature returns to 350°F before you add the next batch.

PECAN CRESCENT ROLLS

With pecans, brown sugar, and cinnamon, these sweet rolls are irresistible.

MAKES 16	INGREDIENTS	MAKES 24
1	egg	1
⅔ cup	milk	1¼ cups
¼ cup	butter	6 tbsp
¼ cup	sugar	6 tbsp
½ tsp	salt	¾ tsp
2½ cups	bread flour	3¾ cups
2 tsp	yeast	1 tbsp
	FILLING	
2 tbsp	very soft butter	3 tbsp
⅓ cup	brown sugar	½ cup
1 tsp	cinnamon	1½ tsp
½ cup	finely chopped pecans	¾ cup

METHOD

Put all dough ingredients in bread pan in order suggested by your bread machine instructions. Set for white or sweet bread, dough stage. Press Start.

When dough is ready, remove it from the bread machine and punch it down. Cut the smaller recipe in two equal parts, the larger recipe into three parts. Let the dough rest for 5 minutes. Oil two or three baking sheets.

On a lightly floured surface, roll out each section of dough into a circle, about 8 inches in diameter. Spread surface with soft butter and sprinkle with mixed cinnamon and sugar, and pecans.

Cut each circle into eight wedges. Starting from the outside of the circle, loosely roll up each wedge toward the point. Stretch slightly and pull it into a curve. Set on the baking sheet with the point underneath.

Let the dough rise until doubled, about 1 hour. Bake in preheated oven 375°F, 12 to 15 minutes.

Apple Kuchen

Kuchen is an easy fruit-filled German coffee cake. This recipe is for an apple topping, but you can substitute soft fruits such as peaches or apricots and skip cooking the fruit before baking.

1 lb LOAF	INGREDIENTS	1½ lb LOAF
1	egg	1
½ cup	milk	⅞ cup
¼ cup	butter	6 tbsp
¼ cup	sugar	6 tbsp
½ tsp	salt	¾ tsp
2 cups	bread flour	3 cups
1½ tsp	yeast	2¼ tsp
	TOPPING	
3 cups	peeled and sliced apples	4½ cups
1 tsp	fresh lemon juice	1 tsp
¼ cup	bread flour or all-purpose flour	6 tbsp
¼ cup	sugar	½ cup
1 tsp	cinnamon	1½ tsp
2 tbsp	butter, softened	3 tbsp

METHOD

Put all dough ingredients in bread pan. Set for white or sweet bread, dough stage. Press Start.

Make the fruit topping while bread machine is working. Pre-cook the apples slightly to soften them. Put them in a saucepan with the lemon juice and about ¼ cup water. Bring water to a boil, then reduce heat and simmer apples, stirring frequently, until they are barely soft, 7 to 10 minutes. Add a little water if needed so apples don't scorch, but there should be as little liquid as possible in the pan when apples are done.

In the meantime, mix the flour, sugar, and cinnamon. When apples are done, toss them with about 3 tbsp of the topping. Mix the softened butter with the rest of the topping. Set apples and topping aside until dough is ready.

Butter a 10-inch round pan (I like to use a springform pan) or a 9-inch square baking pan for the smaller recipe, two 8-inch round pans for the larger one. When dough is ready, remove from pan and punch down. Let it rest 5 minutes. Roll dough out to fit baking pan or pans. Pat the dough into the bottom of the baking pan. Arrange apples on top of the dough. Sprinkle topping over apples. Cover kuchen and put it in a warm place to rise 15 to 20 minutes. Preheat oven to 350°F. (The short rising period will produce a denser, chewier dough. A longer rising period will produce a lighter, more bread-like dough.) Bake kuchen until edges of cake are golden brown, 30 to 35 minutes.

HOLIDAY BREADS

THREE KINGS BREAD

Three Kings Bread, or Rosca de los Reyes, is eaten in Mexico and Puerto Rico on Twelfth Night, January 6, the day the three kings brought Jesus gifts. A tiny ceramic doll, coin, or lima bean may be hidden in the bread. The person who finds it throws a party on Candle Mass, February 2.

1 lb LOAF	INGREDIENTS	1½ lb LOAF
1	egg	1 + 1 yolk
½ cup	water	¾ cup
2 tbsp	powdered milk	3 tbsp
¼ cup	butter	6 tbsp
3 tbsp	sugar	4½ tbsp
2 tsp	grated orange peel	1 tbsp
1 tsp	salt	1½ tsp
2 cups	bread flour	3 cups
2 tsp	yeast	1 tbsp
3 tbsp	chopped walnuts	4½ tbsp
2 tbsp	raisins	3 tbsp
3 tbsp	candied cherries	4½ tbsp

GLAZE

100 g (3½ oz) confectioner's sugar
1 tbsp milk or cream
¼ tsp vanilla

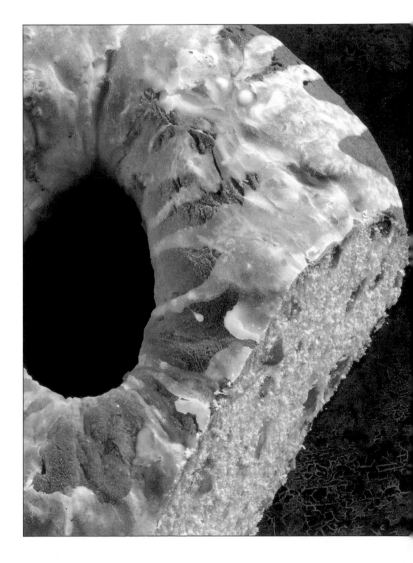

METHOD

Put all dough ingredients except fruit and nuts in bread pan in order suggested by your bread machine instructions. Set for white or sweet bread, dough stage. Press Start. Add fruit and nuts at beeper or after first kneading.

When dough is ready, remove from pan and punch down. Let it rest 5 minutes. Butter an 18-inch baking sheet. Roll the bread into a rope, about 24 inches for larger loaf. Bring ends of the rope together to form a ring, and place bread on baking sheet. Insert a ceramic doll, bean, or foil-wrapped coin into the dough from the underside. Cover dough and put in a warm place to rise until doubled, 45 minutes to 1 hour.

Bake bread in preheated 400°F oven until golden, about 25 minutes.

Make glaze by combining sugar, milk, and vanilla. The glaze should be thin enough to drizzle it, but not runny. Adjust milk if necessary. When bread has cooled slightly but is still warm, drizzle the glaze over the ring.

PAN DE MUERTOS (BREAD OF THE DEAD)

This sweet bread, flavored with orange peel and anise seed and decorated with skull and crossbones, is traditionally eaten in Mexico on the Day of the Dead. This is a day of celebration in Mexico, when relatives honor the dead by visiting their graves and leaving flowers and food there. This bread is shaped and baked in a conventional oven. The dough will fit in either the 1-pound or 1½-pound bread machine.

INGREDIENTS

¼ cup water	½ tsp anise seed
¼ cup milk	3 cups bread flour
2 eggs	1 tbsp yeast
¼ cup butter	1 egg white
¼ cup sugar	2 tbsp water
½ tsp salt	2 tsp sugar
1 tsp grated orange peel	¼ tsp cinnamon

METHOD

Put all but last four ingredients in bread pan in order suggested by your bread machine instructions. Set for white bread, dough stage. Press Start.

Grease a baking sheet. Make an egg wash by mixing the egg white and 2 tbsp water.

When dough is ready, remove it from the bread machine and punch down. Cut off about ⅓ cup of dough. Shape the rest of the dough into a large, round loaf about 2 inches high and place it on the baking sheet. Cut the small piece of dough into thirds. Roll two pieces between your palms to form skinny ropes. Flatten the ends a little so they look like bones. Dip them in the egg wash, then place them on top of the loaf in an X so they look like crossbones. Flatten the remaining piece of dough into a round, then pull it a little to elongate it so it looks like a skull. Dip it in the egg wash, then lightly press it onto the loaf, just above the crossbones. If desired, add tears or facial features.

Brush the loaf with egg wash. Cover the bread loosely. Set it in a warm place to rise until puffy, 30 to 45 minutes. Preheat oven to 375°F. Brush bread again with egg wash. Mix sugar and cinnamon and sprinkle over the bread. Bake until bread is browned and a little crusty, 30 to 35 minutes.

HOT CROSS BUNS

Hot Cross Buns, an English tradition, are eaten on Good Friday. Without the cross, they make delicious breakfast rolls year-round.

MAKES 12 to 16	INGREDIENTS	MAKES 18 to 24
1	egg	1 + 1 yolk
½ cup	milk	¾ cup
¼ cup	butter	⅓ cup
¼ cup	sugar	6 tbsp
1 tsp	grated lemon peel	1½ tsp
½ tsp	cinnamon	¾ tsp
¼ tsp	nutmeg	½ tsp
⅛ tsp	ground cloves	¼ tsp
½ tsp	salt	¾ tsp
2 cups	bread flour	3 cups
2 tsp	yeast	1 tbsp
¼ cup	currants or raisins	½ cup

GLAZE

½ cup confectioner's sugar
1 tbsp milk or cream
½ tsp lemon juice

METHOD

Put all ingredients except currants or raisins in bread pan in order suggested by your bread machine instructions. Set for white bread, dough stage. Press Start. Add the currants or raisins after the first kneading or when the machine signals it's time to add fruit.

Lightly oil a 9-inch square pan or a 10-inch round pan for the smaller loaf, a 9 × 13-inch pan or two 8 × 8-inch square pans for the larger recipe.

When dough is ready, remove from bread machine and punch down. Cut smaller recipe into 12 to 16 equal pieces, the larger recipe into 18 to 24 pieces. Roll each piece into a ball. Place balls about ½-inch apart in baking pan. Cover loosely and set in a warm place to rise until doubled, 45 minutes to 1 hour.

Preheat oven to 375°F. With a sharp knife or razor blade, cut a cross in the top of each roll. Bake 12 to 15 minutes, until a skewer inserted in roll comes out clean.

Make glaze, adding sugar or milk if needed to give it a consistency that will allow you to drizzle it over the rolls but is not runny. Let rolls cool slightly but not completely. Drizzle icing in a cross, following the cuts in the top of the bun.

PANETTONE

This is an Italian Christmas bread distinguished by its tall, domed shape.

1 lb LOAF	INGREDIENTS	1½ lb LOAF
¼ cup	milk	6 tbsp
2	eggs	3
3 tbsp	butter	4½ tbsp
3 tbsp	sugar	4½ tbsp
½ tsp	salt	¾ tsp
1 tsp	grated lemon peel	1½ tsp
1 tsp	vanilla	1½ tsp
½ tsp	anise seed	¾ tsp
2 cups	bread flour	3 cups
2 tsp	yeast	1 tbsp
3 tbsp	pine nuts	4½ tbsp
2 tbsp	golden raisins	3 tbsp
¼ cup	chopped candied fruit	⅓ cup
1 tbsp	flour	1 tbsp

METHOD

Put all ingredients except pine nuts, raisins, fruit, and the last tablespoon of flour in bread pan in order suggested by your bread machine instructions. Set for white bread, dough stage. Press Start.

The high sugar content interferes with the rising action of the yeast, so it is kneaded after the first rising. Remove the dough and punch down. Toss candied fruit with 1 tbsp flour, then gently knead the fruit, raisins, and pine nuts into the dough. Put the dough in a buttered pan and turn so all sides are greased. Panettone is traditionally baked in a tall, cylindrical pan. Use a 1-pound coffee can or a 5-cup soufflé dish for the smaller loaf and a slightly oversized loaf pan or an 8-cup round casserole dish for the larger one. Set it in a warm place, cover loosely, and let rise until doubled in volume.

Bake in preheated 350°F oven until golden and skewer inserted comes out clean, 30 minutes.

LEFT Panettone

CHALLAH

Challah is an egg bread that is oven-baked for the Jewish Sabbath. It is usually a straight, braided loaf, but sometimes the braid is coiled like a snail. At Rosh Hashanah, it may be formed in a circle, symbolizing a prayer rising heavenward.

1 lb LOAF	INGREDIENTS	1½ lb LOAF
2	eggs	3
¼ cup	water	⅓ cup
1 tbsp	butter	1½ tbsp
2 tbsp	sugar	3 tbsp
1 tsp	salt	1½ tsp
2 cups	bread flour	3 cups
2 tsp	yeast	1 tbsp

GLAZE

1 egg yolk
1 tsp water
1–2 tsp poppy seeds

METHOD

Put ingredients in bread pan in order suggested by your bread machine instructions. Set for white bread, dough stage. Press Start.

When dough is ready, remove and punch down. Cut dough into three equal parts. Roll each piece into a rope about 12 inches long for the small loaf, 16 to 18 inches for the large loaf. Braid the three ropes together. Pinch the ends together and turn them under. Cover the loaf and set it in a warm place to rise until doubled in volume, 45 minutes to 1 hour.

Preheat the oven to 350°F. Make glaze by beating egg yolk and water with fork. Brush lightly over loaf. Sprinkle top with poppy seeds.

Bake until top is nicely browned, 30 to 35 minutes.

VANOCKA
(CZECHOSLOVAKIAN CHRISTMAS BREAD)

This is a braided loaf, seasoned with ginger and nutmeg and full of fruit and nuts. It takes some work to knead in the fruit and to make the elegant braids. The loaf is baked in the oven. This recipe will fit both the 1-pound and 1½-pound pans.

INGREDIENTS

⅔ cup milk

1 egg

¼ cup butter

¼ cup sugar

1 tsp salt

¼ tsp ground ginger

¼ tsp ground nutmeg

1 tsp grated lemon peel

3 cups bread flour

1 tbsp yeast

¼ cup slivered blanched almonds

¼ cup golden raisins

1 tbsp candied orange peel

1 egg yolk beaten with 1 tbsp water

2 tbsp sliced almonds

confectioner's sugar

METHOD

Put milk, egg, butter, sugar, salt, spices, lemon peel, flour, and yeast in bread pan in order suggested by your bread machine instructions. Set for white or sweet bread, dough stage. Press Start. You may add the almonds when the machine signals time to add fruit, but don't add the raisins and candied orange peel because the additional sugar in an already sweet bread could interfere with the yeast's rising action.

Oil a baking sheet at least 14 inches long. When the dough is ready, remove and punch down. Knead in the fruit and nuts. Cut the dough into four equal parts. Take three and roll each to form a rope about 18 inches long. Braid the ropes, pinch ends together, and place on the baking sheet.

Cut the remaining piece into four equal parts. Again, take three and roll each between your hands to form a thin rope about 18 inches long. Braid the ropes and center the braid on top of the fat braid. Run wetted fingers along the underside of the thin braid, then lightly press it onto the fat braid. Pinch the ends together and press them under the ends of the fat braid.

Cut the remaining piece into two equal parts. Roll each into a skinny rope about 16 inches long. Twist the two ropes together. Center the twist on the thin braid. Wet your fingers and run them lightly on the underside of the twist, then lightly press onto the thin braid. Pinch the ends together and turn them under. Use four or five toothpicks to skewer the braids in place. Otherwise, the top braids may slip off as the dough rises. Cover bread loosely, put in a warm place, and let rise until dough has almost doubled, about an hour.

Preheat the oven to 375°F. Lightly brush with the egg wash, then sprinkle the sliced almonds over the top and press a few into the sides. Bake until brown and a skewer inserted in a thick part comes out clean. Sprinkle with confectioner's sugar while warm.

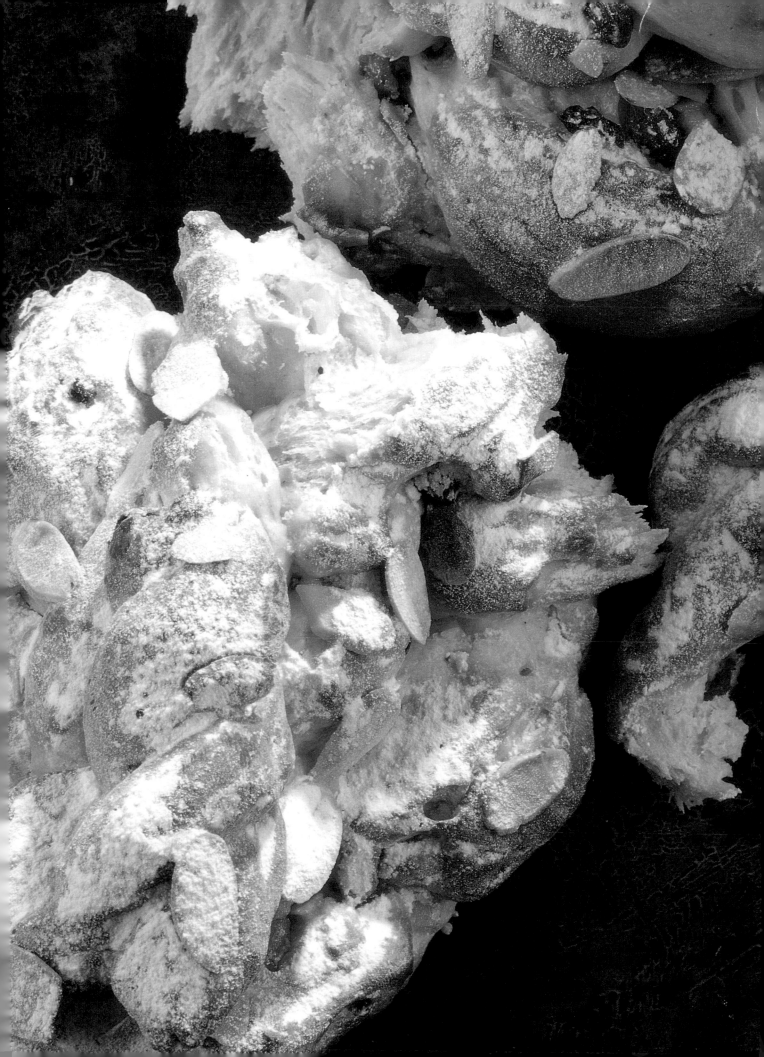

MORAVIAN SUGAR BREAD

Moravian Sugar Bread is a coffee cake that originated in Germany and was brought to the United States by Moravians who settled in North Carolina.

1 lb LOAF	INGREDIENTS	1½ lb LOAF
5 tbsp	milk	½ cup
1	egg	1 + 1 yolk
⅓ cup	mashed potatoes	½ cup
3 tbsp	butter	4½ tbsp
¼ cup	sugar	6 tbsp
½ tsp	salt	¾ tsp
2 cups	bread flour	3 cups
1½ tsp	yeast	2¼ tsp
	TOPPINGS	
¼ cup	brown sugar	⅓ cup
½ tsp	cinnamon	¾ tsp
¼ tsp	nutmeg	¼ tsp
3 tbsp	butter	4½ tbsp

METHOD

Put dough ingredients in bread pan in order suggested by your bread machine instructions. Use a 9-inch loaf pan for the smaller loaf and a 9-inch square baking pan for the larger one. Set for white or sweet bread, dough stage. Press Start.

When dough is ready, remove from bread machine and punch down. Put dough in a greased baking pan and turn so all sides of dough are greased. The mashed potatoes should be plain, with no butter, milk, or seasonings. Cover, put in a warm place, and let rise until doubled in bulk. Preheat oven to 375°F.

Make topping by combining all ingredients in a small saucepan. Heat, stirring often, until butter is melted and sugar is dissolved. With your fingertips, gently make shallow indentations all over the top of the dough. Spread topping across top of bread. Bake 30 minutes.

SWEDISH CHRISTMAS BREAD

This is a dark, dense rye bread made with stout or ale, flavored with orange peel and molasses, and studded with bits of candied orange peel. It is best eaten simply with butter.

1 lb LOAF	INGREDIENTS	1½ lb LOAF
¾ cup	dark stout or ale	1¼ cups
1 tbsp	vegetable oil	1½ tbsp
3 tbsp	molasses	4½ tbsp
½ tsp	salt	¾ tsp
¾ cup	bread flour	1 cup
1½ cups	rye flour	2¼ cups
1 tbsp	grated orange peel	1½ tbsp
2 tsp	yeast	1 tbsp
2 tbsp	candied orange peel	3 tbsp

METHOD

Put all ingredients except candied orange peel in bread pan in order suggested by your bread machine instructions. Set for whole-wheat bread, medium crust. Add candied orange peel after first kneading or when beeper indicates time to add fruit.

GREEK NEW YEAR'S BREAD

This bread, slightly sweet and flavored with orange, is traditionally eaten on New Year's Eve. The baker hides a coin in the bread, and the person who finds it will have good luck in the new year, according to Greek tradition.

1 lb LOAF	INGREDIENTS	1½ lb LOAF
1	egg	2 + 1 yolk
⅓ cup	milk	½ cup
¼ cup	butter	⅓ cup
¼ cup	sugar	6 tbsp
2 tsp	grated lemon peel	1 tbsp
2 tsp	grated orange peel	1 tbsp
½ tsp	salt	¾ tsp
2 cups	bread flour	3 cups
2 tsp	yeast	1 tbsp

GLAZE

1 egg white beaten with 2 tsp water
2–3 tbsp pine nuts
(you may substitute slivered almonds)
1–2 tbsp sugar

METHOD

Put all dough ingredients in bread machine pan. Set for white or sweet bread, dough stage. Press Start.

When dough is ready, remove from pan and punch down. Let it rest 5 minutes. Butter a baking sheet. Roll the bread into a rope, about 30 inches for smaller loaf, about 40 inches for larger loaf. Coil the rope into a circle on the buttered baking sheet. Insert a foil-wrapped coin into the dough from the underside, where it cannot be seen. Cover dough and put in a warm place to rise until doubled, 45 minutes to 1 hour.

Brush dough with egg-water wash. Stick pine nuts in the folds of the dough, following the circular pattern. Sprinkle with sugar.

Bake bread in preheated 375°F oven until golden, about 30 minutes.

INDEX